LEAD WITH A STORY

LEAD WITH A STORY

RICH CAVAGNARO

CONTENTS

TESTIMONIALS

With a heart as big as his smile, Rich Cavagnaro connects with everyone he encounters, and his unwavering belief in them transforms lives.

R. Josef

A truly endearing and inspiring person who is generous, kind and genuine. Always looking for smiles and creating happiness. Grateful for his friendship 🧡🥰

M. Pierson

This book demonstrates the kind of leader Rich is, forward thinking, inspirational, creative and a child at heart!

C. Spencer

An entrepreneur who always put his family first, while striving to be a success. Proof you can do both.

J. Melofchik

A combination of intelligence, confidence, and kindness, Rich Cavagnaro is a role model in all walks of life. He is a successful entrepreneur and mentor, a loving and devoted husband and father, and the truest of friends.

D. Walsh

Rich Cavagnaro has an exceptionally high emotional IQ. He genuinely cares about others and their well-being. I have never seen anyone who so unselfishly gives to others... whether it is a kind word or giving support to those in need or creating a positive work culture. He is a rare gem and a true blessing to all of those who know him.

C. Condon

Rich is the most genuine, creative, out of the box thinker I have ever met. He consistently challenges and encourages others toward achieving goals they would otherwise think weren't attainable.

R. James

I have never met anyone more creative and more generous than Rich. He truly enjoys bringing the best out of people. He has been a mentor and a father (away from home) to me, and he has mastered the art of enjoying life.

P. Araya

When I find myself in times of trouble, I call Rich.

R. Padraigh

Rich Cavagnaro is a joyful, smiling soul in a world filled with frowners. He has a rare ability in understanding who people are and what they need often before they do themselves, a level of observation that has given him a masterful insight into the world of business and beyond. Rich spent his child-hood moving rocks, but he now sits atop a mountain built by compassion, love, and family: and boy is it sunny at the top!

J. White

FOREWORD

Family is not just about blood ties, but about the bonds we forge through with shared experiences, laughter, and tears. Growing up (and still do), I had the privilege of witnessing my brother's creativity, imagination, and perseverance firsthand in many different experiences.

As I read through the pages of this book, Lead with a Story, I couldn't help but feel an overwhelming sense of pride and awe at the person my brother has become today. His writing is a testament to his talent, dedication, and passion for storytelling and inspiration.

I'm honored to call Richard my brother and to have had the privilege of watching him bring this project to life. I know that you, the reader, will be just as moved and inspired by his stories as I have been with this book.

As you turn the pages, I hope you'll experience the same sense of wonder, insight, and connection. My brother's book has the power to inspire, to comfort, and to challenge us to see the world in new and unexpected ways.

Congratulations, brother, on this remarkable achievement. I'm honored to be a part of your journey.

Nancy McManus

Sister and Friend

PREFACE

During a Christmas break, I bought a book on Aesop Fables. I hadn't read any Aesop Fables since perhaps fourth grade. However, references to different stories and the memories accumulated during the years always stayed with me. I enjoyed the use of a metaphor to tell a story and the moral that went along with it. I particularly remember fourth grade because I won a contest on my created Aesop Fable-like story. I don't recall what my story was, it has long been lost to history and even makes the fact that the collection of Aesop Fables that have been recorded extremely memorable and valuable. Upon reading that book, so many lessons still apply to this day, and that in itself can be concerning because we are supposed to learn from history. It struck me that I could provide an opportunity to tell stories with a lesson and put it into a more modern flair of storytelling.

Every journal starts with a single word. What I envision

with this book is a weekly reflective journal for aspiring business leaders. I share a story that perhaps is known for which a leader can use in a business setting to teach or emphasize a point and then I add a personal experience that I relate to that story. There are no rules or right answers to my comparison it just is a point that somehow connects for me. I then ask the reader to reflect on the stories and answer a few questions. I share 52 stories in this book with the intent that you choose one story a week to consider. The desire is by reflecting on personal experiences you will be better prepared for the challenges you face as a business leader, parent, family member, or friend. I share some personal and business stories, some are successes, other's failures, some are highs, and some are lows. What I hope you take away from my stories is life is challenging and also rewarding. Don't be fooled by not believing that others have easy lives all the time, recognize that life requires you to accept sorrow and defeat but through character building, perseverance and awareness many joyful moments can occur as well. So, enjoy the weekly lessons and answer them honestly when you can go a little bold, have some fun, and move yourself forward. And if you feel that you would like to share a story with me or perhaps seek a lending ear or advice please reach out to me.

1

BE HAPPY

There was once a boy who hardly had any toys or money. Nevertheless, he was a very happy little boy. He said that what made him happy was doing things for others and that doing so gave him a nice feeling inside. However, no one really believed him; they thought he was loopy.

He spent all day helping others, dispensing charity to the poorest, and looking after abandoned animals. Very seldom did he ever do anything for himself. One day, he met a famous doctor who thought the boy's case was so peculiar that he decided to investigate him. So, with a complex system of cameras and tubes, the doctor managed to record what was happening inside the boy. What he discovered was surprising.

Each time the boy did something good, a thousand tiny angels gathered around the boy's heart and started tickling it. That explained the boy's happiness, but the doctor continued studying until he discovered that we all have our own thousand angels inside us. Unfortunately, he found that, as we do so few good things, the angels spend most of their time wandering about, bored.

And so, it was that the secret to happiness was discovered. Thanks to that little boy we now know exactly what we have to do to feel our hearts being tickled.

My Story

Several years ago, I was asked to come into my wife's third-grade class to speak on career day. My wife asked me to speak to the kids because I am the CEO of a company I started. After speaking to the class about what it's like to be an entrepreneur, I asked the kids "what they wanted to be when they grew up?" I had answers from doctors, engineers, teachers, and professional athletes and one wanted to be President. However, one blond-haired blue-eyed girl's answer stopped me in my tracks and quite literally changed my life. Her answer to the question, "to be happy." She recently moved to the U.S. from Israel and I couldn't help reflecting on the tension that exists in Israel with the conflict with the Palestinians. Imagine if it was left up to this girl to lead the negotiations and how things might be able to turn out differently for everyone. I took this girl's suggestion and branded it as my company's Core Culture philosophy. I stumbled upon a Danish word, "arbejdsglaede," which translates to "Live Happy at Work" and made this our Company mantra. Our performance as a company has improved dramatically since we adopted this change, sales have increased by 20% year over year for three years in a row, profits have quadrupled, and employee retention is over 95%. I believe these results are a direct link to Arbejdsglaede and Arbejdsglaede is a direct link to the student in my wife's class. On that day I visited my wife's classroom, the experienced entrepreneur went back to school and learned a valuable lesson from one of the students, so from now on when I'm asked what I do, I say I'm not a CEO but instead a CHO, Chief Happiness Officer!

Moral

Sometimes the teacher is the student.

Reflection

How open are you to learning from someone generationally younger than you?

Have you had opportunities to provide reverse mentoring to persons older than you? How did that go?

Have you had any experiences where you pivoted from an entrenched belief? Describe the situation.

Have you had any experiences where you made someone pivot from their entrenched belief? What happened?

---

https://freestoriesforkids.com/children/stories-and-tales/origin-happiness

How does being happy impact your decisions?

____

____

____

What is an action you can take this week to give knowledge or get knowledge?

____

____

____

For more information on Arbejdsglaede, see the wonderful book Leading by Happiness by Alexander Kjerulf, of Woohoo Inc.

2

TWO CATERPILLARS

Two caterpillars were sitting on a leaf eating lunch and having a chat. Suddenly they heard a loud swishing noise and could feel a current of air whooshing past them. Looking up, they saw a beautiful butterfly flying overhead. The first caterpillar looked to the other, shook his head, and said, "You'll never get me up in one of those things."

I can relate this story to a situation we faced in the company when it was time to move out of our initial 1,800-square-foot office. My business partner was reluctant to increase our space beyond 3,000. ft. We had a similar discussion to that of the caterpillars. I persuaded him to see that we can't grow the company if we confine our space, or put another way, we need to escape from our cocoon and spread our own wings. We took 5,000sq. ft, then two years later took the adjoining 5,000sq.ft., then a few years later another 7,500 sq. ft. Since then, we are now in 33,000sq. ft and now are looking to double our space again.

Moral

You cannot become a butterfly by remaining a caterpillar. Change happens and when it does view change as positive.

Reflection

How have you at times been like the caterpillar?

____

____

____

Do you know anyone who is like the caterpillar?

____

____

____

How aware are you or your co-workers of change or do you ignore it like the caterpillars?

____

____

____

The butterfly represents change, what do you consider to be a change-worthy sign for you?

____

____

____

Caterpillars don't fly, and the story assumes they may fear flying. What fears might you need to address to undergo your metamorphosis?

____

____

____

In the coming week, write down a few things that you fear

or things that are holding you back. What are 1-2 actions you can take to change yourself forward?

____

____

____

Story from Scott Simmerman, 1997

3

BIG BROTHER ELEPHANTS

Elephants in so many ways share interesting traits with human beings. One overlapping area is mentoring young elephants. Over the course of the last few decades, it has been observed that young elephants throughout Africa have been known to search out and kill rhinos for no apparent reason. Park rangers decided to institute a "big brother" program that paired young elephants with older elephants with the hope it would prevent the troubled teens from acting up. Incredibly enough the program worked, and rhino deaths have gone down.

I was the young elephant early in my career and would charge hard against those who were in front of me. It wasn't until a boss gave me the book, How to Win Friends & Influence People by Dale Carnegie that I changed my ways. While in no way would I call my former boss an elephant 😊, she took me under her tutelage and provided a more successful approach to dealing with others. Ultimately, I achieved even better results and had a much happier time doing it.

Moral

Teaching others goodness is noble, or Success is all about growing others

Reflection

Mentoring programs are a common tool companies can use to onboard new employees faster. What mentoring is available in your company/school?

____

____

____

Have you ever participated in a mentoring program? Were you the mentored or the mentor? What was the situation?

Many of us are introduced to the concept of Coaching from playing sports, how can your career benefit from having a "big brother"? What area of career improvement would you be interested in seeking mentoring?

So many situations in the workforce can benefit from "big brother" programs. What actions can you take this week that can stop your office rhino deaths?

4

MERRIER CHRISTMAS

It was a sweltering day with the sun overhead when birds and animals could find very little to drink to quench their thirst. Among them was a thirsty crow who searched for water all over the fields. He looked everywhere, but there was not a drop to drink.

He felt weak and sad and thought to himself, "Caw, caw, caw. I have been searching for water since the morning, but there is not a drop in sight!" "The thirst is making me dizzy."

Just as the crow was glooming, he suddenly saw a water pitcher. "Thank goodness! I hope there is some water in that little pitcher."

He flew straight down to that pitcher to see if water was left in it. And to his surprise, there was some water in the pitcher.

As the crow pushed his head into the pitcher, it could not go deeper. "Oh no. I could not get to the water." The pitcher was high with a narrow neck, and the water level was too low. He tried pushing the pitcher to a side for the water to flow out. "If I tilt this pitcher, maybe the water would come out, and I will easily drink it." But the pitcher was very heavy to tilt.

The crow did not lose hope. He looked around and started thinking of a way to get water out of the pitcher. Then, an idea struck him! He saw some pebbles on the ground. The crow started collecting pebbles one by one and dropped them into the pitcher. As more and more pebbles went into the pitcher, the water rose up. Soon enough, the water came to a level through which the crow could drink water. He drank the water happily and thanked mother nature.

When I started my Company, finances were tight for several years, in fact didn't take a paycheck for almost one year. This put a lot of strain on Christmas since our family has always celebrated the holiday in a "Griswold" over-the-top way. To compensate for not having any disposal income, I set out to create an atmosphere of low-cost events to enhance the holiday spirit. One event was when we split up and created two teams, my two younger sons on my team and my wife and older son on the other. Each team received $20 for decorations and we had a Christmas tree theme decorating contest. Over the years we had PoeTrees, and AncesTrees, when my father past, we had in his honor a "My Favorite Things" tree, many wonderful creative ideas, and much time spent doing crafts helped create some holiday magic. We also spent time making up games, a tissue box tied around your waist filled with 1-inch size bells and you had to race to empty the tissue box of all bells, we called this Jiggle Bells. Another popular game was The Stockings Were Hung, in this game you put a tennis ball in a pantyhose leg and put the pantyhose on your head, twelve dollar store nutcrackers were set up like a clock and you had to stand in the middle of the clock and knock over the nutcrackers in the quickest time. Prizes for these games and many others were typically lottery tickets with the hope we could win $100,000 or more in a prize. Since gifts were scarce, we often had to do some interaction questions before opening a gift, it may be to write down your favorite

Christmas tune, movie, cookie, or gift, or possibly call a relative before opening a gift. All these activities ended up building more joy into our Christmas season and these traditions have carried on as my sons are all adults. Sharing this story is important for many reasons, one, financial discipline is required at different times in your life and these periods of hardship can frame who you and your family become. Secondly, in my opinion, the commitment one must make to their career must not replace or consume the commitment you have to your family or oneself first.

Moral

Necessity is the mother of all invention, No one ever spent time on their deathbed wishing they spent more time in the office.

Reflection

Have you recognized the need in your personal finances to have a disciplined financial plan? What areas need more attention or planning?

____

____

____

Have you had instances where the dual priorities of work and life are intersecting causing some strife? If so, what happened and what was the result?

____

____

____

Can you recall a hardship you experienced and how that has ultimately provided you with personal growth? Explain.

____

____

____

Describe your ideal work-life balance. How close are you to achieving that balance?

____

____

____

What steps can you take this week to identify actions you can take to enhance your work-life balance?

____

____

____

P.S. For a complete list of Christmas and/or Thanksgiving games and activities, email me at rcavagnaro129@icloud.com

5

DON'T CROW ABOUT IT

Crows can remember human faces, and apparently, if they don't like you, they won't forget you either. Scientists who trapped some crows for research made this discovery when the crows would constantly heckle them whenever they walked into the lab. By using masks, they came to realize that the crows actually held a grudge against the people who had trapped them. Interestingly enough, the children of the crows would later carry on the same grudge. *

Often, we harbor the same feelings as human beings, we can easily hold grudges against those who have harmed us, and rightfully so. But at what point must we learn to let go so we are not dragged down by this invisible force? As managers we set the tone for our staff on how to act when we have been wronged, we also can influence the future behaviors of our staff and not cloud their vision. We faced a similar experience in the company when a merger we were involved with failed miserably. We were able to unravel the merger over time, but it almost cost us our company. Many people including me were bitter and when we would come across some of our former colleagues it was easy to squawk. However, we turned our focus on what we had to do to execute our goals and soon enough the grudge was forgotten.

Moral

Let go or be dragged. Your vision determines your future

Reflection

How are you like the Crows? Who do you harbor a grudge against? Is it time to let go? What would need to occur to let it go?

____

____

____

What situations have you been in where you were influenced like the children of the crows?

____

____

____

Have you passed along a grudge to others? Explain

____

____

____

Can you identify a situation where you accepted an outcome and moved forward? Explain

____

____

____

What actions can you take this week to create a different vision for a situation that is pulling you down?

*Source Wikipedia

6

MAN OF LAMANCHA (2020 UPDATE WOMAN OF LAWOMANCHA)

A young man in his twenties was seeing out from the train's window shouted,

"Father, look at the trees! They are going behind!" The young man's father smiled at the man, and a young couple sitting nearby looked at the young man's childish comment with pity. Suddenly, the young man exclaimed again. "Father, look at the clouds! They are all running with us!" The couple couldn't resist and said to the old man. "Why don't you take your son to a good doctor?" The older man smiled and said, "We did, and we are just coming from the hospital. My son was blind from birth, and he just got his vision today." Every person in the world has a story. Don't judge people before you truly know them. The truth might surprise you.*

Early in my management career, I was provided with a tremendous gift from a boss. He sent me to a weeklong Executive Compression Lab for me to learn how to handle and manage stress. The course deprived participants of regular meals, and sleep and threw difficult but realistic management challenges at the 20 or so attendees. The course paralleled the well-known book by Alexander Dumas on the quest of Don Quixote who faced extreme criticism as he attempted to perform chivalrous acts for the downtrodden and destroy the wicked. Almost all participants emotionally broke down during the week, as the instructors pulled from critiques they had with our co-workers or family from pre-event surveys or from videos of working group sessions from the event. I often was surprised to see some

---

*   (Source: https://alltimeshortstories.com/short-stories-about-life/)

people I had projected to be manager superstars succumb at times to being overwhelmed or handling people poorly especially when fatigued. The instructors used the breakdowns to then begin building individuals back up. I was able to perform well during the week and it provided a level of confidence that I could handle stressful situations that were bound to happen. Throughout my career of owning my company and dealing with many unforeseen challenges, I was constantly able to pull from that experience to keep me steady during difficult times. I am Irish & Italian so I was already challenged with Keeping Calm and all the help I could get was like nectar! As uncomfortable as that training was to face criticism from peers and family it laid an important foundation for me to become the type of manager(person) I am.

Moral

Smooth seas don't make skilled sailors
> Master your feedback, master your momentum

Reflection

Recall a time in your life when you received criticism. What were the circumstances? Was the criticism justified?

Have you ever received feedback from a supervisor or coach that helped you improve? Explain.

We all are on a journey, how are you preparing yourself to succeed?

Do you have a mentor? Can you identify a person whom you feel would be a good career mentor/coach? If so, take action and ask them, if not. begin your own quest to find someone.

If you are unfamiliar with the song, The Impossible Dream by Richard Kiley from the Broadway play about Don Quixote called Man of La Mancha, listen to it and feel the inspiration.

7

THE AMERICAN DREAM

A man came to America from Europe, and after being processed at Ellis Island, he went into a cafeteria in New York City to get something to eat. He sat down at an empty table and waited for someone to take his order. Of course, nobody did. Finally, a man with a tray full of food sat down opposite him and told him how things worked.

"Start at that end." He said, "And just go along and pick out what you want. At the other end, they'll tell you how much you have to pay for it."

"I soon learned that's how everything works in America; Life is a cafeteria here. You can get anything you want if you're willing to pay the price. You can even get success. But you'll never get it if you wait for someone to bring it to you. You have to get up and get it yourself."

This story resonates on so many levels, my family came to the U.S. through Ellis Island, and as a child, I could look out my bedroom window and see the Statue of Liberty, so it's no surprise somewhere in my mind all the way back to my childhood that when I went to sleep, I would have the "American Dream." I realized when starting my own company, "You have to get up and get it yourself." Yes, I have had to pay the price, and so has my family and while we have had help along the way, it's always been don't wait for others...go make it happen.

Moral

For those who wait...move aside or "Without action, you aren't going anywhere" Gandhi

Reflection

Recall a recent situation where you were waiting for an outcome to occur before taking action. Explain.

____

____

____

Recall a story where instead of waiting you got up and made something happen.

____

____

____

When you were a child what was your dream for your future self?

____

____

____

What is your Dream? What are you doing to make it happen?

____

____

____

What can you do over the next week to act toward a successful endeavor?

____

____

____

Source *Bits & Pieces

8

DON'T QUIT

If you want to learn about somebody who didn't quit, look no further than Abraham Lincoln. Born into poverty, Lincoln was faced with defeat throughout his life. He lost eight elections, twice failed in business, and suffered a nervous breakdown!

Here is a Sketch of Lincoln's Road to the White House:

"1816" His family was forced out of their home... He had to work to support them!

"1818" His mother died!

"1831" Failed in business!

"1832" Ran for state legislature and lost!

"1832" He also lost his job! He wanted to go to law school but couldn't get in!

"1833" Borrowed some money from a friend to begin a business and by the end of the year he was bankrupt! He spent the next 17 years of his life paying off this debt!

"1834" Ran for state legislature again and won!

"1835" Was engaged to be married, sweetheart died, and his

heart was broken!

"1836" Had a total nervous breakdown and was in bed for six months!

"1838" Sought to become speaker of the state legislature and was defeated!

"1840" Sought to become elector and was defeated!

"1843" Ran for Congress and lost!

"1846" Ran for Congress again and this time he won! He went to Washington and did a good job!

"1848" Ran for re-election to Congress and lost!

"1849" Sought the job of land officer in his home state and was rejected!

"1854" Ran for Senate of the United States and lost!

"1856" Sought the Vice-Presidential Nomination at his Party's National Convention and got less than 100 votes!

"1858" Ran for U.S. Senate again and again he lost

"1860" Elected President of the United States!

I certainly don't want to match the record of losses and failures that President Lincoln experienced however, I do share some overlapping history and while I wasn't born into poverty, I did have very humble beginnings as I was one of four siblings with my dad supporting the family on a lone teacher salary.

"2010" We lost our supply contract which represented almost 80% of our revenue.

"2011" Merged with another company but that company lost its revenue opportunity

"2013" Had a failed business merger

"2013" Lost our Banking Line of Credit

"2014" Lost ownership control of my company

"2014" Lost control of the Board

"2015" Lost over $300K in revenue owed to me from the merger settlement

"2015" Lost control of my salary & bonus structure

"2020" Purchased back the Company and WON complete control!

"2021" Sold the Company to a large public firm and retired young.

. . .

Abe could have quit many times, but he didn't, and because he didn't quit, he became one of the Greatest Presidents in the history of The United States of America! Lincoln was a Champion and he never gave up! I too never gave up and hopefully can claim to be the Greatest President in my Company's history! 😉

Moral

Don't quit before the miracle happens.

How does this story relate to your life?

____

____

____

How do you think Abe Lincoln was able to persevere?

____

____

____

What setback have you had that required perseverance to overcome?

____

____

____

Can you think of other examples of people who have overcome setbacks to achieve a successful outcome?

____

____

____

What situation are you currently engaged in that you fear may have a negative outcome? What actions can you take to lead to a positive outcome?

____

____

____

9

—————

THE BOULDER

In ancient times, a King had a boulder placed on a roadway. He then hid himself and watched to see if anyone would move the boulder out of the way. Some of the king's wealthiest merchants and courtiers came by and simply walked around it. Many people loudly blamed the King for not keeping the roads clear, but none of them did anything about getting the stone out of the way. A peasant then came along carrying a load of vegetables. Upon approaching the boulder, the peasant laid down his burden and tried to push the stone out of the road. After much pushing and straining, he finally succeeded. After the peasant went back to pick up his vegetables, he noticed a purse lying in the road where the boulder had been. The purse contained many gold coins and a note from the King explaining that the gold was for the person who removed the boulder from the roadway.

This story resonates with a personal experience with my company. When I started the company, I had a sublicensing agreement with a U.K. company based in the U.S. However, the material we were purchasing was manufactured by a large German chemical company that had an agreement solely with the U.S. company. The material we were purchasing was used to remove a contaminant from the drinking water and was only produced by the German manufacturer. Over the years my company was constantly removing the big boulders in the road only to see our licensing "partner" take credit for growing the market. Eventually, over time (10 back-breaking years) the German company came to realize we were doing all the heavy lifting and decided to sell to us directly. For my company, this was like finding the purse with the gold coins, as we were able to lower our Cost of Goods dramatically and we were no longer handcuffed to competing against our "partner." Our efforts to grow the market and outwork our competition and "partner" directly led to our success

Moral

Every obstacle we come across in life gives us an opportunity to improve our circumstances, and whilst the lazy complain, the others are creating opportunities through their kind hearts, generosity, and willingness to get things done.

What life experience have you had that is relatable to this story?

____

____

____

What boulders have you removed as a teenager or young adult that helped pave the road ahead for you?

____

____

____

What difficult situations have you faced in the past where you observed the lazy behaviors of others?

____

____

____

Have you been surprised by creating goodwill for others by volunteering yourself to help with a task?

____

____

____

What actions can you take this week to remove a big boulder that is blocking your growth?

____

____

____

10

———

THE OLYMPIAN

Wilma Rudolph certainly didn't get any head start in life. She was the twentieth of twenty-two children born into a poor family in Tennessee. In childhood, she fell victim to polio and was forced to wear leg braces until she was nine. At the age of 12, she tried out for her school's girls' basketball team. She failed.

But for the next year, she practiced virtually every day with a girlfriend and two neighborhood boys. The next time around, she made the team. It soon became evident that she could get from one end of the court to the other quicker than anyone. A college track coach spotted her and talked her into letting him train her to be a sprinter. Her prowess earned her a scholarship to Tennessee State University. Where she became a track star.

In 1960, she made the U.S. Olympic team. In the 100-meter sprint, she had to face Yetta Mynie of the German team. Yetta was unbeaten and the world record holder in that event. Wilma won. She did it again in the 200-meter event. Wilma's third race was in the 400-meter relay, in which she ran the anchor leg. Yetta Mynie was also running the last leg. Just as the baton was handed to Wilma, she dropped it, giving Yetta the lead. Her never-give-up spirit made her pick up the baton and take off in desperate pursuit. She caught the German champion in the last few strides and won a third gold medal, more than any other woman at that time.

For a year Wilma Rudolph traveled the country telling her life story. "I let them know," she says, "that they can achieve, that they can grasp anything they want to grasp as long as they are willing to work for it."

This is the story of my life and my company. I have often felt confident in my leadership and sales abilities but less so in my financial aptitude. I have had to work at developing those skills and have been defeated a few times. One of the most stinging setbacks was at the urging of my Board and

Unitholders that I needed to hire a CFO for the company. A selection was made with the Board's acceptance and shortly thereafter when he reported financials everyone was happy except for me. He was reporting financials that used spreadsheets and templates and sentence verbiage that made everyone believe the numbers were trustworthy, I had other tools that I relied upon and were telling a different story. After 6-9 months, I objected to the declining cash flow and debt situation fired the CFO, and had to lay off almost 10% of my staff to keep the company afloat. So yes, I dropped a baton by allowing the CFO to have more reporting authority but realized the desperate situation I was in and quickly recovered the company to put us on a winning path. Incidentally, I hired another CFO and this time I didn't have the Board participate in the hiring process.

Moral

Miracles often happen after hard work. Or Setbacks are a prerequisite for success

How does this story relate to a life experience that you have had?

____

____

____

Reflect on a situation where you needed to work hard to improve a skill. What was involved? What was the outcome?

____

____

____

Think of a situation where you have had to come from behind to win. Was it a game, a sporting event, or a situation at school or work? Describe the situation.

____

____

____

Describe a situation where you had to overcome a setback, what occurred?

____

____

____

What actions can you take this week to improve a skill in need of improving?

____

____

____

11

THE MILER

Sir Roger Bannister was the first man to run a mile in under four minutes. Up until he did it in 1954, most people thought the four-minute mark was impossible to break. They thought the human body couldn't physically go that fast – that it would collapse under the pressure.

No one could run a mile in less than four minutes. It was impossible. *You were crazy to even try.*

In the 1940s, the record for running a mile had reached 4:01. But it hadn't budged since. Some doctors and scientists said it was physically impossible to run a mile in less than four minutes. Not just hard, or dangerous, but impossible.

Bannister decided to do it – to run a mile in less than four minutes. Bannister's chance came on May 6th, 1954. Bannister had finished in 3:59.4

He'd done what so many believed was impossible. He'd made history.

Once Bannister proved that it was possible to run a mile in under four minutes, suddenly everyone was able to do it in fact within a year 6 other people broke the four-minute mile!

The odds of having a start-up company survive 1 year is 10%, the odds of a start-up company exceeding $ 1 million in sales is less than 1%, and Exceeding $20 Million is even lower less than 0.1% however, while those odds would scare many people from starting up a company it can happen. Each time we passed a sales milestone we set a greater goal and while the first million was the hardest each milestone deserves celebrating. We are not done setting sales records and now we know we can do what we previously thought was impossible.

P.S. As of today the mile record is 3:43. I wonder if a 3-minute mile is possible! 😊

Moral

Once you stop believing something is impossible, it becomes possible.

Can you think of an individual feat that you thought was impossible only to see otherwise? Why did it happen?

____

____

____

What obstacle have you overcome that you at one time thought was insurmountable?

____

____

____

What is something ahead of you that you find to daunting a challenge? What actions can you take toward accomplishing the impossible?

____

____

____

In this story, it is quite surprising that within the year of the impossible happening, six other people broke the 4-minute mile. How can you relate this to an experience in your life?

____

____

____

12

THE COMPETITOR

Talk show host Larry King tells this story about Ty Cobb. When Cobb was 70, a reporter asked him, "What do you think you'd hit if you were playing these days?"

Cobb, who was a lifetime .367 hitter, said, "About .290, maybe .300."

The reporter said, "That's because of the travel, the night games, the artificial turf, and all the new pitches like the slider, right?"

"No," said Cobb, "it's because I'm 70."

If you are a fan of baseball or not, you can enjoy Ty Cobb's response. If you don't sense this from the exchange Ty Cobb was fiercely competitive. My staff views me the same way. Whenever we have any company games, whether horseshoes, foosball, ladder ball, or cornhole I have a drive and skill level to win at these games, much to the annoyance of my staff! It's quite possible that I may gloat a little. My company organized an Olympics event of minute-to-win type games. Teams were selected and it was clear from the first event the competitive juices to keep my team from winning was in play. After the event and much arguing over rules which seemed to be ever-changing so my team couldn't win, we finished up in second place. Much to my surprise I was awarded pre-made Second Place medals immediately after the event. So, they had their joke! However, I lodged a formal protest!

While seemingly a simple example I have always appreciated the desire of people to compete. This is a valuable trait that I believe employees should possess. It is this inner drive that helps people succeed at their goals. When hiring people, I look to assess their competitive spirit, and while it is not of course the only trait I look for it is important.

Moral

Bring your game, not your name

How do you assess your competitive spirit? Do you hate losing more than you like winning?

____

____

____

Have you ever been surprised by a competitive result you received? What happened?

____

____

____

When looking at your co-workers or new hires, how do you assess their competitive drive to succeed at their work or goals?

____

____

____

In reviewing your company or department goals, what are some actions you can take this week to position yourself or the company to achieve the goal destination?

The Best of Bits & Pieces, 1994, pg 33

13

CONFIDENCE

The following is a poem that Arnold Palmer had on a wall in his home.

If you think you are beaten, you are.
If you think you dare not, you don't.
If you'd like to win but think you can't,
It's almost certain that you won't.
Life's battles don't always go

To the stronger woman or man,
But sooner or later those who win
Are those who think they can.

What strikes me about this poem is Arnold Palmer one of the golfing greats still needed to be reminded to have a winning attitude. Confidence is such a multiplier of productivity. In my career as a business leader, nothing I could ever do was as impactful to increasing productivity in my team as positive encouragement. I remember once going to a conference I was slated to speak at, and I had a young staff engineer on my team with me. I suggested to my colleague that she could deliver the presentation. At first, she balked but after some more nudging, she went ahead and did it. This experience boosted her confidence so much that the timid engineer eventually rose in the ranks of the company to be our Latin America Business Development Manager.

Moral

Inhale confidence, exhale doubt

Henry Ford once said, "Whether you think you can or can't, you're right." How does this quote reflect your life story?

____

____

____

Reread the poem, stop and pause on each line, and think how that line applies to you either in the present or the past.

Having trust in yourself or your skills is really having confidence in yourself. What do you expect from yourself? What do you think is possible? Do you just go for it or do you hold back?

____

____

____

Who do you know that can provide you encouragement? Take some time this week to reach out to that person and pinpoint some areas of your life or career that need a productivity boost.

____

____

____

14

———

THE BLIND MAN AND THE
ADVERTISING

Warning: This story contains language and a potentially 'offensive stereotype' of a visually impaired person that certain audiences may find objectionable. At the same time, the story carries a powerful main message, is culturally/historically significant, and is useful in debating equality/disability, aside from its obvious 'different perceptions' theme. So be careful how you use this story. Alter the language appropriately where warranted, position it carefully, and if in doubt do not use the story at all. This story is not recommended for education/sharing unless you are very sure of how to use it safely.

An old blind man was sitting on a busy street corner in the rush hour begging for money. On a cardboard sign, next to an empty tin cup, he had written: 'Blind - Please help'.

No one was giving him any money.

A young advertising writer walked past and saw the blind man with his sign and empty cup, and saw the many people passing by completely unmoved, let alone stopping to give money. The advertising writer took a thick marker pen from her pocket, turned the cardboard sheet back-to-front, and re-wrote the sign, then went on her way.

Immediately, people began putting money into the tin cup. After a while, when the cup was overflowing, the blind man asked a stranger to tell him what the sign now said.

"It says," said the stranger, " 'It's a beautiful day. You can see it. I cannot.' "

I remember a negotiation I was involved with for a key raw material we needed. We were negotiating for a lower price if we purchased more material. The negotiation had reached an impasse as my supplier would not budge. We decided to change the discussion away from the price of goods to one of how many lives we could impact at various price points. By reframing the discussion, we were able to get a substantial price reduction and yes be able to impact more people globally.

Moral

See the opportunity in every difficulty

Take a few moments and think about the difficulties facing those who experience disabilities, discrimination, or equality. Who do you know who faces these challenges?

____

____

____

Some people may find this story offensive, could it be retold in a less offensive way?

____

____

____

The choice of words is so critical to our communication with others, do you have an example where the words you used were either offensive or propelled a conversation forward?

____

____

____

Can you think of an advertising slogan or commercial that you believe is a powerful message?

____

____

____

What are some actions you can take this week that can help you reframe a challenge that you face?

____

____

____

Watch the YouTube video at this link: https://youtu.be/ Hzgzim5m7oU

15

HE'S NOBODY'S FOOL

When Albert Einstein was making the rounds of the speaker's circuit, he usually found himself eagerly longing to get back to his laboratory work. One night as they were driving to yet another rubber-chicken dinner, Einstein mentioned to his chauffeur (a man who somewhat resembled Einstein in looks & manner) that he was tired of speechmaking.

"I have an idea, boss," his chauffeur said. "I've heard you give this speech so many times. I'll bet I could give it to you."

Einstein laughed loudly and said, "Why not? Let's do it!"

When they arrived at the dinner, Einstein donned the chauffeur's cap and jacket and sat in the back of the room. The chauffeur gave a beautiful rendition of Einstein's speech and even answered a few questions expertly.

Then a supremely pompous professor asked an extremely esoteric question about anti-matter formation, digressing here and there to let everyone in the audience know that he was nobody's fool. Without missing a beat, the chauffeur fixed the professor with a steely stare and said, "Sir, the answer to that question is so simple that I will let my chauffeur, who is sitting in the back, answer it for me."

In business, we are always excited to see confidence in our staff and we want to push people forward. A similar experience happened to me once when I was scheduled to give a talk at a tradeshow on the removal of arsenic from drinking water. A member of my team was itching to show she could grab the podium and give the talk. I happily obliged and the talk went wonderful...until the Q&A part. Having already been aware of this metaphor story I was prepared and when I could see the level of questions had exceeded my employees' comfort zone, I gracefully joined her at the podium to answer questions. Several lessons were learned that day, the obvious one was to show trust in an employee, but also to demonstrate I will help carry an employee if they falter my employee also learned to gain more knowledge before taking the stage.

Moral

Every expert was once a beginner.

How have you experienced a similar story in your life or your career?

____

____

____

Do you have the courage to act like the chauffeur? Do you have an example?

____

____

____

Speaking is an audition for leadership, do you have any opportunities where you could create an opportunity to give a talk or a webinar? How would this help your career?

____

____

____

What actions can you take this week to gain more knowledge about your work responsibilities or opportunities so you can be better prepared for a Q&A?

____

____

____

16

———

THE CHINESE FARMER

There's an old story about a Chinese farmer whose horse escaped into the mountains. When his neighbors expressed their sympathy for his bad luck, he told them, "Bad luck? Good luck? Who knows?"

Soon the horse returned with a herd of horses to the village. When the neighbors congratulated the farmer on his good luck, he told them, "Good Luck? Bad luck? Who knows?"

The farmer's son worked to break the horses but fell and broke his leg. When the neighbors expressed their sympathy for his bad luck, he told them, "Bad luck? Good luck? Who knows?

While his son was healing, the army came and conscripted every able-bodied young man in the village. Since his son was not taken the neighbors congratulated the farmer on his good luck, he told them, "Good luck? Bad Luck? Who knows?

In 2018 President Trump issued tariffs on imported steel and aluminum, immediately U.S. producers of steel raised their prices accordingly and our profits dipped immediately as we were forced to eat these price increases. I could hear the words in my head, "Good Luck? Bad luck? Who knows?" Shortly after this the economy started heating up and our business was growing at a good clip, we needed to hire more staff to keep up but couldn't find experienced workers, "Good Luck? Bad luck? Who knows?" We then had excessive-quality performance issues cutting into our profits and retooled operations and operating procedures. "Good Luck? Bad luck? Who knows?" After this the Coronavirus hit and impacted the supply chain of parts from China, fortunately, due to the steel tariffs of two years earlier we had shifted away from our dependency on China-produced materials, so "Good Luck? Bad luck? Who knows?"

Moral

Life is not a single scene. It's a whole movie and our only challenge (or opportunity) is we don't know what comes next.

Can you think of a similar experience you have had as it relates to this story?

____

____

____

When have you experienced bad luck only to look back over time and see it as good luck?

____

____

____

Has luck played a role in your career? If so how?

____

____

____

The Harder I work, the luckier I seem to be. How does this quote relate to you?

What actions can you take this week with an ongoing situation that will put you on a path to avoid bad luck or good luck?

EVERYBODY, SOMEBODY, ANYBODY, AND NOBODY

This is a little story about four people named Everybody, Somebody, Anybody, and Nobody.

There was an important job to be done and Everybody was sure that Somebody would do it.

Anybody could have done it, but Nobody did it.

Somebody got angry about that because it was Everybody's job.

Everybody thought that Anybody could do it, but Nobody realized that Everybody wouldn't do it.

It ended up that Everybody blamed Somebody when Nobody did what Anybody could have done.

After about five years, the company had grown to about fifteen employees. We started reaching a point where our teamwork started to break down and problems among employees were rising. Something needed to be done. I organized an off-site retreat meeting for two days and we held our first Strategy Meeting. The meeting was guided by Patrick Lencioni's book, The Five Dysfunctions of a Team. I encouraged everyone to criticize any issue we have as a company but avoid any personal attacks. For some of the prep, I changed the roles of staff and we did some improvisation examples to illustrate certain teamwork gaps. Folks had to don wigs, wear certain style clothes, assume different nationalities, be parents, be happily married, be unhappily married, etc. to really mix things up. I tried to encourage everyone to be a little uncomfortable in their role. The mock scenarios demonstrated that communication is so important for a team to thrive and we cannot possibly judge individuals until we understand the shoes they wear. A dozen or so years later, we still have a handful of employees who were with the company for that event, and it is still company folklore.

Moral

Teamwork makes the dream work

Can you think of a team you have been on that has not functioned effectively? Explain?

____

____

____

Conversely, have you participated on a team that seemed to gel? Explain, then compare to the previous question.

____

____

____

What are a few questions you can ask of your peers to help you become a better teammate?

____

____

____

What can you do in the coming week to improve the performance of a team you participate in or the performance of your staff or co-workers?

18

THE MARKETER

Three stores on the Main Street in town stood side by side. They all sold the same type of merchandise. One day the owner of the store at one end put up the sign: ROCK-BOTTOM PRICES.

This prompted the storekeeper at the other end to hang up a sign reading: LOWEST PRICES IN TOWN.

The owner of the store in the middle was thrown by these

aggressive maneuvers until he had a bright idea. He put up his own sign, which proclaimed, MAIN ENTRANCE.

I have always enjoyed being creative and believe a second career at an advertising company would have been a good alternative career fit. In 2002 the U.S. EPA lowered the allowable level of arsenic in drinking water in drinking water. Much controversy was swirling around on whether it was the right thing to do, was the level low enough, or whether should it have been higher. Many states started efforts to comply with the new standard and many found ways to delay any implementation. One state that moved forward more aggressively than others was New Hampshire. I was traveling to NH often back in that time as we were trying to enter the market with a new technology to remove arsenic from drinking water. I couldn't help but see over and over again on NH license plates the motto, "Live Free or Die." We used that motto, to release our first print advertisement which showed an NH License plate with our six-letter company name on the plate, but we altered the motto to, "Live *Arsenic* Free or Die."

Moral

B DFFRNT

Sylvia Simmons-*How to Be the Life of the Podium.*

Looking back over your life what is something that you are particularly proud about with something you have created?

____

____

____

Can you think of an advertisement that you particularly enjoyed? What made it unique?

____

____

____

What are some of the options you could consider doing if you were the two merchants on the end?

____

____

____

Inspiration can come from many different exercises, what is a particularly challenging situation you face in the coming week for which you can bring about a creative approach?

____

____

____

For more on this topic of creativity, look into the

THINKPAK by Michael Michalko author of *Thinker Toys,* or the *Creative Whack Pack* by Roger von Oech.

19

THE TRAVELER

A traveler nearing a great city asked a man seated by the wayside, "What are the people like in the city?"

"How were the people where you came from?"

"A terrible lot." The traveler responded. "Mean, untrustworthy, detestable in all respects."

"Ah," said the sage, "you will find them the same in the city ahead."

Scarcely was the first traveler gone when another one stopped and also inquired about the people in the city before him. Again, the old man asked about the people in the place the traveler had left.

"They were fine people; honest, industrious, and generous to a fault. I was sorry to leave," declared the second traveler.

Responded the wise one: "So you will find them in the city ahead."

The story makes me relate to the following quote from Clement Stone who has hung in my office for close to twenty years, "There is little difference in people, but that little difference makes a big difference. The little difference is attitude. The big difference is whether it is positive or negative."

In 2011, I made my first trip to Africa and attended a U.S. Commercial Service trade event in South Africa. The trip happened to be the largest-ever US trade event in Africa. U.S. Commercial Services from every African country that the U.S. had embassies in attended the event. Naturally, I was excited to see a new continent and a new country. I arrived in the late evening and took a shuttle to my hotel where the event was planned. The days of the event happened to coincide with the tenth anniversary of 9/11. At breakfast the next morning, the conference organizers announced that a terrorist threat had been received for the event. So, they were going to enforce a lockdown for all foreign visitors, and we were not allowed to leave the hotel grounds. We were provided with safety procedures if anything occurred. Well, my five-day trip to South Africa allowed me to become very intimate with a large US. owned hotel. On the last day, I decided to check out early and I had the hotel secure me a driver so I could spend my day driving around Johannesburg. I ended up getting a driver who was older in age and had been aligned with Nelson Mandela when he was a youth and during the 1970s was active in protesting against Apartheid. He took me all over the city and the surrounding geography on a five-hour drive. We saw Nelson Mandela's property, visited the slums downtown, and several overlooks above the city. We passed a poverty-stricken area built on an old gold mine dump site, which still happened to be mined for gold. My driver was extremely proud of his city and I got two gifts that day: one from the drive and sightseeing, but also from his friendly storytelling. I found the driver to be "honest, industrious, and generous to a fault. I was sorry to leave."

Moral

It's your attitude that makes you.

When you think about this story, can you think of a similar life experience?

____

____

____

Who do you know can provide you with wisdom like the sage in the story?

____

____

____

We all face challenges in life, can you think of a situation where you observed either a negative or positive attitude by the participants and what was the outcome?

____

____

____

What actions can you take this week to shift your thoughts to a positive attitude on a particularly difficult challenge you face?

____

____

____

Bits & Pieces

20

THE WOODPECKER

I magine renting a rustic wooden cabin in a beautiful forest setting for your honeymoon. The place is delightful. At dawn, however, a woodpecker starts its rat-a-tat pounding on the roof. The noise was so loud you couldn't sleep. It happens at dawn the second morning, again on the third morning, and so forth. What could you do?

Many people say they'd shoot the bird. Some say, "Who cares? It's your honeymoon."

This incident with a woodpecker happened to Gracie and Walter Lantz on their honeymoon. They were a happy, playful couple and they discovered an opportunity. By the time they had returned from their honeymoon, they were inspired to create the cartoon character "Woody the Wood-pecker." Walter was the illustrator, and Gracie the voice. Many years later, when interviewed on their 50th wedding anniversary, Gracie said, "It was the best thing that ever happened to us."

Early in my professional career, I was given an opportunity to transfer out of my homegrown state of New Jersey and move to Ohio. My wife and my entire family were almost all located in NJ. My wife and I decided to take on the experience. We learned why it was concerning to leave our families, our marriage was strengthened and the friendships we made were impactful as we moved into a new neighborhood with lots of young families. We never shed a tear when we moved from NJ but three years later, we had to relocate back to NJ and the emotions to leave were staggering. In retrospect, we learned from the experience the desirable ideal way we wanted to raise our family and while we lived in a beautiful area of NJ, we struggled to make our finances and lifestyle match what we had in Ohio. I had over an hour commute one way on a good day, and with three boys I was missing a lot of quality parent time. An opportunity arose to move to Atlanta and years later I was able to be able to start my own company. If I stayed in NJ, this would never have been possible.

Moral

Pay attention opportunity may be knocking when you least expect it.

Can you think of a time when a disruption in your life actually turned out to be a benefit?

____

____

____

We all have "noise" in our life. What is something that you wish you could quiet? What would you need to do to make that happen?

____

____

____

Upon reflection, can you think of a scenario where you had a pivotal decision to make and chose to take the predictable comfortable one? Do you think life would have turned out differently if you chose a different path? How?

What is something you can do this week that you can benefit from by taking an action you have been postponing?

THE SAVE

I heard a story once from a friend about going back to the old days of coin-operated phones in the airport. He had called his wife and said "good-bye" and hung up the receiver. He had taken only a step or two and the phone rang. He figured it was the operator telling him he owed more money for the call.

In fact, it was the operator. But instead of asking for more money, she said, "Sir, I thought you would like to know that after you hung up, your wife said she loves you."

I had a similar experience once when I won an award as the Small Business Entrepreneur of the Year for the Metro Atlanta Chamber of Commerce. I had been nominated to be in the finals for the award and the night before at dinner, my sons asked if I had a speech in case I won. I said no way was I going to win. The people I was up against were brilliant: one was working on a cancer drug, one had a healthcare business and created hundreds of jobs, another was developing fuel cells, etc. But for the rest of dinner, I said, "I would thank all those who helped me except for my wife because she really could have done more to help me out." We all had a good laugh, except, of course, my wife! Well, when they announced the winner with all the finalists on stage, I was shocked to hear my name called the winner. When I spoke, I thanked everyone who helped, even my banker who was in the room… but I forgot to thank my wife!!! As I sat down, I realized my error and jumped back on stage grabbed the mic from the emcee, and said, I had one more person to thank, my wife. I remember hearing someone yell out, "Nice Save!"

Moral

It's never too late to do the right thing.

Can you recall a situation where you either did not acknowledge a person you should have or were late to do so?

———————————————————

———————————————————

———————————————————

We sometimes need a second chance; can you recall where you were provided a second chance? What happened and what was the result?

———————————————————

———————————————————

———————————————————

Can you think of a situation where you had the opportunity to do the right thing...did you do it or did you blow it?

———————————————————

———————————————————

———————————————————

What is something you can do this week to act on communicating with someone who you feel you should acknowledge for their efforts to assist you?

———————————————————

———————————————————

———————————————————

22

THE 7% SOLUTION

According to author, Kate Murphy in her book *You're Not Listening*. It turns out that the words we use play a surprisingly small role in our overall communication. It's widely thought that at least 55% of the emotional content of a spoken message is transmitted nonverbally through things like facial expression and body language. And tone of voice conveys 38% of someone's feelings and attitudes. This means that the words we use account for just 7% of our overall communication.

So, what can we do about it? For starters, refrain from gazing out a window or checking your phone while listening to someone—you might miss important nonverbal cues. In fact, keeping your phone tucked away and attending more to face-to-face interactions might boost your nonverbal listening skills. In one study of children at a device-free outdoor camp, researchers found that after just five days without phones or tablets and interacting with their peers, the kids were able to accurately read facial expressions and identify the emotions of people in photographs and videotaped scenes significantly better than controls who had not attended the camp and continued using their devices.

But it's equally important to monitor your own nonverbal signals while you're listening. To encourage more open and honest communication, try adopting what Murphy calls the listener's demeanor, which involves a calm expression that transmits interest and acceptance. The eyes don't dart or wander away, the fingers don't fidget, and the body seems relaxed and open, which means no crossed arms or legs. With the listener's demeanor, there is no indication that you're on a schedule, or that there's somewhere else you'd rather be.

It's remarkable how many times in my professional life, I have had to make sure that I repeat a message multiple times before it sinks in. One example was prior to the COVID-19 event, I struggled to get my staff to understand the urgency to eliminate repeatable mistakes my company makes. Correcting them always seems near the bottom of people's to-do list. After the outbreak, we had a company video call and I demonstrably used strong inflection and said, "We either get better now or we become a much smaller company." People finally found the purpose to listen, and I couldn't afford only seven percent communication! All my facial expressions and body language were sent and received.

Moral

Listen with your eyes as well as your ears

Go back and reread this story, what did you miss the first time you read it? What did you miss the first time?

____

____

____

Recall a recent situation when your attention drifted, and you missed some details.

____

____

____

Can you recall a situation where you were not listened to at the expectation you had hoped for?

____

____

____

What meeting will you be attending this week where you can practice active listening?

____

____

____

23

AND THEN SOME

A retired business executive was once asked the secret of his success. He replied that it could be summed up in three words- "and then some."

"I discovered at an early age," he declared, "that most of the difference between average people and top people could be explained in three words. The top people did what was expected of them--and then some."

"They were thoughtful of others; they were considerate and kind—and then some. They met their obligations and responsibilities fairly and squarely—and then some. They were good friends and helpful neighbors—and then some. They could be counted on in an emergency—and then some."

I am thankful for people like that for they make they make the world more livable. Their spirit can be summed up in the three little words, "and then some."

During the COVID-19 situation, I was fortunate to have built a company culture that I could see my team rally around the concept of...: and then some." We had staff members voluntarily travel to start-up systems in the heart of hot spots. We had staff tackling several goals that needed actions dusted off of them. We had salespeople learn to communicate through video chats with clients. We introduced several new service programs. We launched new quality programs. We started lean manufacturing initiatives. We had our shop floor work four days at ten hours a day and there are many more examples. Those three little words were differentiators to AdEdge and were used for content on our digital media platforms to showcase our company culture. Our digital media traffic had a ridiculous monthly growth of over five hundred percent during the COVID-19 outbreak. It's because of this philosophy of three little words that AdEdge was able to grow our sales pipeline for the future by millions of dollars during an imperious economic slowdown.

Moral

The EXTRA ingredient is.... YOU!

Can you think of a situation where you went the extra mile? How did you feel? What was the outcome?

____

____

____

Describe a situation where you did just enough and left your best effort a little short.

____

____

____

Can you recall a co-worker or supervisor who constantly puts forth a better-than-expected effort? How does it feel to be around such a person?

____

____

____

What is something on your to-do list for the coming week where you can provide a little extra?

____

____

____

From Even More of the Best of Bits & Pieces

24

LEAD A HORSE TO WATER

The sales trainee was trying to explain his failure to close a single deal in his first week. "You know," he said to his manager, "you can lead a horse to water, but you can't make him drink."

"Make him drink?" the manager sputtered. "Make him drink? Your job is to make him thirsty."

Often, I had times when I was knocked off the purpose of what I was all about with my company. I remember a time when just the opposite happened to me and I had a young salesperson remind me that. It was our purpose that made our customers thirsty. One of the core values of our company was a "Passion for Clean Water." We were conducting a sales meeting for our forecast for the coming year, and I was pushing the team hard to come up with a robust growth plan. We had our technical literature in place, we had PowerPoint presentations, we had case studies that discussed the technical improvements we achieved, and we even had a video testimonial from the customer touting the benefits and ease of use of our system. The young salesperson pointed out all that stuff is great to have but the reason the person on the video choked up was because after many years she was finally thirsty because she was drinking water that no longer had arsenic in it! Point made to me as well, and my thirst was recharged as well Incidentally that young salesperson soon became my VP of Sales!

Moral

People with Passion change the world.

I shared this story with a young co-worker who spent time doing charity work in Kyrgyzstan, and she replied, "I like the story and I like the moral, but I gathered from the story that the moral is more than just passion. Seeing other's passion for things does make it more exciting, but I think the greater challenge is figuring out how to drive others to share in that passion. When you are thirsty/passionate for a change, you need to figure out how to make others thirsty/passionate for that change."

This story actually reminded me of our time overseas working in villages. We learned in community development that you must figure out what their "felt need" is. We could teach them all day about why they "need" clean water, but if they don't "feel" that need, then they will not care when the system falls apart. Sometimes we found out their "felt need" was not for clean water to drink, but for growing better crops.
"

Recall a time when you applied for training that you received, what was the situation and how did you apply it?

____

____

____

Think back to a situation you have faced that knowing what you know now you would have handled things differently.

____

____

____

Can you think back to a time when you witnessed a moment unfolding in front of your eyes that you knew would become a future story that you could tell?

____

____

____

What is something that you can work on this week where you can change the delivery of how you have been going about your work and reframe the situation where you make someone thirsty?

____

____

____

From Even More of the Best of Bits & Pieces

A LACONIC ANSWER

(From The Book of Virtues)

Long ago the people of Greece were not united, as they are today. Instead, there were several cities and states, each with its own leader. King Philip of

Macedon, a land in the northern part of Greece, wanted to bring all of Greece together under his rule. So, he raised a great army and made war upon the other states, until nearly all were forced to call him king. Sparta, however, resisted.

The Spartans lived in the southern part of Greece, an area called Laconia, and so were sometimes called Lacons. They were noted for their simple habits and their bravery. They were also known as people who used few words and chose them carefully; even today a short answer is often described as being "laconic."

Philip knew he must subdue the Spartans if all of Greece was to be his. So, he brought his great army to the borders of Laconia and sent a message to the Spartans. "If you do not submit at once," he threatened them, "I will invade your country. And if invade, I will pillage and burn everything you hold dear. If I march into Laconia, I will level your great city to the ground."

In a few days, Philip received an answer. When he opened the letter, he found only one word written there.

That word was, "IF."

Many times in business, you have ideas and often don't act on them. I had a situation where I was contemplating such a scenario early in our company's history. We had an agreement with our key supplier of material to not only purchase the material we used to remove arsenic in drinking water but also the system for which it was deployed. We faced repeated problems with the quality and schedule to have systems supplied to us, so one day I had the thought that if we built our own systems we could control our destiny better. We approached our supplier and after a few discussions over several months, they agreed. Our ability to grow the company clearly was boosted by making this change. "If" is such a small word but it has big ramifications, it takes a little courage and bravery to turn such a small word into a powerful asset.

Moral

Never underestimate the value of courage

Think of a time in your life when you can finish the sentence, "If I...."

____

____

____

Can you think of a time when you lacked the courage to act? What was the situation?

____

____

____

Can you think of a time when you did demonstrate courage? What was the situation?

What is something in the coming week, where you can demonstrate a little more courage?

THE FAIRY

A couple were dining out together celebrating their 40th wedding anniversary. After the meal, the husband presented his wife romantically with a beautiful very old gold antique locket on a chain.

Amazingly when his wife opened the locket, a tiny fairy appeared. Addressing the astonished couple, the fairy said, "Your forty years of devotion to each other has released me from this locket, and in return, I can now grant you both one wish each - anything you want.."

Without hesitating, the wife asked, "Please, can I travel to the four corners of the world with my husband, as happy and in love as we've always been?" The fairy waved her wand with a flourish, and magically there on the table were two first-class tickets for a round-the-world holiday.

Staggered, the couple looked at each other, unable to believe their luck.

"Your turn," said the fairy and the wife to the husband.

The husband thought for a few seconds, and then said, with a little guilt in his voice, "Forgive me, but to really enjoy that holiday of a lifetime - I yearn for a younger woman - so I wish that my wife could be thirty years younger than me." Shocked, the fairy glanced at the wife, and with a knowing look in her eye, waved her wand.....

and the husband became ninety-three.

When we make wishes or even lay out strategic goals for a business, we often start off in one direction but end up somewhere else. Many years ago when I was living in NJ and experienced a winter with over 100 inches of snow, I said enough and interviewed for a job with a company headquartered in Atlanta. I was driven around parts of the northern suburbs of Atlanta and was immediately captivated by the difference from NJ. All the homes, buildings, and stores were recently built. The interview went great and a few days later I was offered a job in Tampa! Tampa did not have the same appeal to me, I wanted to get away from snow but still enjoyed having Spring and Fall. It was not for another decade until a situation arose that allowed me to relocate to the Atlanta area.

(Adapted from a suggestion from J Riley.)

Moral

Of course, the cliché "Be careful what you wish for" comes to mind.

Think of a wish that you have had, has it come true yet?

____

____

____

We often wish for something but end up with unintended consequences, can you recall such a scenario for yourself or for someone you know?

____

____

____

We often start our careers and must zig and zag to get to

the spot we want to be, what is the long-term plan you envision for yourself?

____

____

____

What is something you can do this week to take steps in the direction of making your dream come true?

____

____

____

SCHOOL

A mother repeatedly called upstairs for her son to get up, get dressed, and get ready for school. It was a familiar routine, especially at exam time.

"I feel sick," said the voice from the bedroom.

"You are not sick. Get up and get ready," called the mother, walking up the stairs and hovering outside the bedroom door.

"I hate school and I'm not going," said the voice from the

bedroom, "I'm always getting things wrong, making mistakes, and getting told off. Nobody likes me, and I have got no friends. And we have too many tests and they are too confusing. It's all just pointless, and I'm not going to school ever again."

"I'm sorry, but you are going to school," said the mother through the door, continuing encouragingly, "Really, mistakes are how we learn and develop. And please try not to take criticism so personally. And I cannot believe that nobody likes you - you have lots of friends at school. And yes, all those tests can be confusing, but we are all tested in many ways throughout our lives, so all this experience at school is useful for life in general. Besides, you must go, you are the head-teacher."

Hopefully, you saw the joke and not yourself in the story! It is tough to learn how to take criticism. As a business owner, I have faced pride and obstinance to think my ideas are not the best ones. I still can regrettably fall into this trap. I used to get myself worked up for my annual shareholder meetings, I had inherited my unit holders from a bad merger. We were not aligned, they invested in the company I merged with on the belief they had struck gold. Well, that business went belly up, but my side of the business held on and eventually reached breakeven status. The investors now had a chance to see an exit strategy. The unitholder meetings were never about our strategies to grow the company they wanted an exit. I remember bringing my passion to the meetings only to be met with cranky country club know-it-alls who knew nothing about the water industry and how slow it takes to launch products. Over time, my company flourished, and I was able to buy them out. Although it's one of my proudest achievements, and I was able to pass the many difficult tests that I had to take, I sometimes struggled to get out of bed to conduct Board meetings and Unitholder meetings but I'm sure glad I got up.

(Based on a suggestion from P Hallinger.)

Moral

We grow stronger by being tested or Get up, make your dreams happen

What has been a challenge you faced that overwhelmed you?

____

____

____

What was a challenge you overcame? What did you have to do to accomplish that outcome?

____

____

____

What is one of your career fears? What steps can you take to start preparing yourself to overcome this fear?

———————————————————————————

———————————————————————————

———————————————————————————

What challenges wait for you this week that you have been putting off and keep you from jumping out of bed in the morning? Who would be a good mentor for you to work with to overcome this challenge?

———————————————————————————

———————————————————————————

———————————————————————————

28

THE SHOPPING CART

(Idea came from a sentence in Hunch by Bernadette Jiwa)

One night, after observing that customers stopped shopping when their baskets became too heavy or too full, Sylvan Goldman contemplated a problem begging for a solution. In 1936, he sat in his Humpty

Dumpty supermarket chain office wondering how customers might purchase more groceries. He found a wooden folding chair and put a basket on the seat and wheels on the legs. Goldman and one of his employees, a mechanic named Fred Young, began tinkering. Their first shopping cart was a metal frame that held two wire baskets. Since they were inspired by the folding chair, Goldman called his carts "folding basket carriers." The cart was awarded a patent on April 9, 1940, titled, "Folding Basket Carriage for Self-Service Stores." He advertised the invention as part of a new "No Basket Carrying Plan."

The invention did not catch on immediately. Men found them effeminate; women found them suggestive of a baby carriage. "I've pushed my last baby," an offended woman informed Goldman. After hiring several male and female models to push his new invention around his store and demonstrate their utility, as well as greeters to explain their use, shopping carts became extremely popular and Goldman became a multimillionaire. [4] Wikipedia

My company faced a similar dilemma when we were exporting drinking water treatment systems to Chile. We had to reserve space on ocean containers and because the systems we built were in sizes irregular to ocean containers we had to pay extremely high freight rates that negatively impacted our sales possibilities in international markets. We came up with an idea to help lower costs to build our treatment systems to fit inside an ocean container and called them WaterPods, soon thereafter we started making sales. Little did we know the problem we solved for international shipments became a product of choice in the U.S. Engineers and communities were able to get WaterPod containers in different lengths and different outside veneers to blend into a community. The WaterPods also offset higher building costs to house a treatment system saving communities additional money. And while I'm not a millionaire, I am Rich. 😉

Moral

See opportunities not problems

Recall a problem you have had and a creative solution that was applied to solve the problem.

____

____

____

What is a good idea that you have seen recently from a company or entrepreneur that solved a problem?

____

____

____

What is a problem that you have that is in need of a creative solution? Who can you ask for ideas on how to solve the problem?

What actions can you take in the coming week to address a repeated problem that you have in your work/life? Imagine you are Thomas Edison, Albert Einstein, Elon Musk, Jerry Seinfeld, Oprah Winfrey, or on SharkTank how would they solve the problem?

29

THE MONEY HUNTER

(From Hunch by Bernadette Jiwa)

Roger Pasquier doesn't own Apple shares, but he has clearly profited from the smartphone revolution. Before he retired, Roger was an ornithologist: for thirty years he has also been a money hunter who collects dropped coins and bills from New York pavements.

Pasquier has been keeping records of his haul since 1987. From then until 2006, his average annual total was $58. Since 2007, when Apple launched the iPhone, he has averaged $95 a year. It stands to reason that people staring at their screens don't notice a spare change in the gutter.

Pedestrians have become so immersed in their smartphones that the city of Sydney is trialing in-ground traffic lights in an attempt to cut pedestrian deaths on the city's roads (sixty-one pedestrians were killed on New South Wales roads in 2015; that is up 49 percent from 2014)

Distractions and focus surround us every day. I have been to Israel twice both times I got to mix pleasure and business and I have mostly enjoyed the experience. I take away the vitality that Israelis have for enjoying life in the moment. However, the two times I have been to Tel Aviv separated by around 4 years between visits, rocket alarms have gone off and were intercepted by the Israeli Defense Force. I have been told that my two trips were the only times in the past four years for the alarms to go off! Jokingly Israelis have told me to consider not returning. Not being used to hearing alarms and casually taking cover as Israeli citizens do is quite a distraction and easily gets you to lose your focus. My Israeli colleagues were able to go about business within minutes of the alarms going off and yet it took me a little longer to reset! While this is a legitimate distraction, I too can be distracted by my phone and need the discipline to not succumb to the habit of looking at my phone and focusing on seeing my surroundings. When I coached a youth baseball team one of the habits I had to instill in the players was to go through a mental checklist before every pitch, know the count, know how many outs there are, know where the baserunners are, anticipate if a ball is hit to you what play you can make, anticipate if the ball is hit hard or soft, a pop-up or line drive. I never had the most talent on my team, but I did have a team that executed above their level because they were better able to focus.

Moral

Starve your distractions, feed your focus

What mishap have you had in your life because you were distracted?

____

____

____

Think about a situation where you have experienced both distractions and focus. What happened?

____

____

____

We often can do our best work by being focused, describe a time when this occurred for you.

____

____

____

This week you will have many distractions, but what is one thing you commit to focusing on that you will benefit from?

____

____

____

30

IS THIS YOUR BEST

shutterstock.com · 2170605027

Compiled from <u>Power Questions</u> by Andrew Sobel & Jerold Panas

The following is a story told by Winston Lord who was a special assistant to Secretary of State Henry Kissinger.

Henry Kissinger asked Lord to write a foreign policy report to give to President Nixon. Lord knows Kissinger is very demanding and expects his best work, but even Lord is unprepared for what happens next. Lord himself tells the story.

I developed a good draft of the policy report and turned it into Kissinger. He calls me the next day and says, "Is this the best you can do?"

I say, "Henry I thought so, but I'll try again."

So, I go back in a few days with another draft. He calls me in the next day and he says, "Are you sure this is the best you can do?"

I say, "Well, I really thought so. I'll try one more time." Anyway, this goes on eight times, eight drafts; each time he says, "Is this the best you can do?"

So, I go in there with a ninth draft, and when he calls me in the next day and asks me the same question, I really get exasperated and I say, "Henry, I've beaten my brains This is the ninth draft. I know it's the best I can do. I can't possibly improve one more word."

He then looks at me and says, "In that case, now I'll read it." *

Lord eventually went on to become the US Ambassador to China.

I remember feeling the same way when writing the business plan to start my company. I had a mentor at the time that made me go through a similar exercise. My original business plan was over sixty pages. After much red ink and suggested deletions of unnecessary information it was reduced to around twenty pages. I often had extra words and sentences that provided no additional context to the business plan. I still find myself today hearing him say, "Less is more." And while I'm still guilty at times of overcommitting to more words, I try to remember this lesson.

Moral

"Best is good, better is best" or Less is more (More or less! ☺)

When have you been guilty of completing work or a project and knew you likely could do better?

____

____

____

Who in your life has held you to a higher standard of excellence?

____

____

____

Think back over the last week and recall a project you were involved in and ask yourself if in fact, "Is this the best I can do?"

What is something coming up in the current week that will demand your best effort? Are you ready to give your best?

---

*Source   www.gwu.edu/~nsarchiv/coldwar/interview/ episode-15/lord1/html.

NON UM PAR

The etymology of umpire comes from Latin. As we know, the task of an umpire is to treat the players equally. In Latin, this is expressed as UM PAR. Since the umpire is supposed to be above the players, he was called none-UM PAR which in Latin is NON-UM PAR. There are several expressions in English that were restructured due to confusion having to do with the indefinite article. The indefinite article "a" is used when a word begins with a consonant sound and "an" when a word begins with a vowel sound. This rule proved confusing for the hearer if he did not know a new expression in English. For example, the original word for orange was "orange." When one asked for an orange, they said "A norange." This was confusing to the hearer who perceived it as "an orange." The same thing happened to the word umpire. The expression "a numpire" was heard as "an umpire," and the word was restructured, and lost the initial consonant "n." *

I wanted to share this story because the understanding of a word's derivation is interesting to me. Coming up with a name for a company or a product is sometimes a fascinating journey. The first name of our product to remove arsenic remove was AD33, we took the AD from the type of technology we used called Adsorption. Adsorption is a chemical process that relies on the adhesion of one material to another. The 33 comes from the atomic weight of arsenic on the periodic table. After we launched the product, I was shortly thereafter at a trade show when a customer came up to me and expressed surprise, that my company had named a product AD33. I rubbed my head in puzzlement until he expanded that was the year Jesus was crucified...oops! We quickly changed the name of the product.

Moral

Taste your words before saying them

All of us at times have either been surprised to learn a word's meaning or misapplied a word correctly, can you think of when this has happened to you?

———————————————————————————

———————————————————————————

———————————————————————————

Can you think of a product that you can identify as a perfect name?

———————————————————————————

———————————————————————————

———————————————————————————

Can you think of a description of a brand that has become a replacement for the word itself? For example, Kleenex with Tissue

———————————————————————————

———————————————————————————

———————————————————————————

This week, think of something your company does either

as a service, a process, or a product that you can suggest a
name to brand it.

____

____

____

Source: https://web.uri.edu/iaics/files/M.-LAKHWANI-R.-
CLAIR.pdf

ALEXANDER THE GREAT HORSERIDER

Philip, Alexander's father, bought a horse called Bucephalus for an exorbitant price, but the rambunctious animal bucked all comers. Watching the futile attempts, Alexander noticed that the animal was frightened by its own shadow. He bet his father that he could mount the horse. By turning Bucephalus toward the sun so its shadow was behind it, Alexander was able to climb into the saddle and gallop around triumphantly. To which his father said: "My boy, you must find a kingdom big enough for your ambitions. Macedonia is too small for you." Of course, we are not talking about just any Alexander, we are sharing a story about Alexander the Great. And what made Alexander, "The Great" was a combination of being educated by Aristotle, and being curious but also being bold.

Henry David Thoreau once said, "It's not what you look at that matters, it's what you see." Alexander was able to see that his horse was afraid of its shadow even though everyone else saw a horse that looked like it could not be tamed.

My relatable experience to this story was once when I went to a GA Tech Engineering Poster Board event for students to share with potential hires a project they had worked on. I was greeted by a young engineer who did not have a poster in the event, but I was impressed by her communication and grace in directing visitors throughout the exhibit. After walking around the event and finding a half dozen or so students that we wanted to interview, I set my sights on the engineer who greeted me. No one else "saw" her because she was a host, I succeeded in getting her to consider employment with my firm although she had some other options. When she said yes to working at my company, like Alexander I galloped around triumphantly. Years later, I am still joyful that I hired Alexandria The Great!*

*Her name was changed ☺

Moral

To quote Alexander the Great, "Fortune favors the bold."

We all have examples of not being able to see something that others saw, what is your story?

____

____

____

Can you think of a situation in your life where you were watching something and then saw something unfold in front of you before others were able to observe it?

____

____

____

The well-known quote "Fortune favors the bold" has been around for centuries, how can you apply that quote to your life?

____

____

____

In the coming week, what is something you can benefit from by not just looking at but actually stopping and seeing?

____

____

____

Excerpted from <u>Moralstories26</u>

HOW TO WIN FRIENDS & INFLUENCE PEOPLE

(From the book of the same title by Dale Carnegie)

As Abraham Lincoln was dying, Secretary of War Stanton said, "There lies the most perfect ruler of men that the world has ever seen." What was the secret of Lincoln's success in dealing with people? Historians refer back to a time when Lincoln was a young man in Pigeon Creek Valley of Indiana. He not only criticized others, but he wrote letters and poems ridiculing people and dropped these letters on country roads where they were sure to be found. One of these letters aroused resentments that burned for a lifetime.

In the autumn of 1842, he ridiculed a vain pugnacious politician by the name of James Shields. Lincoln lampooned him through an anonymous letter published in the Springfield Journal. The town roared with laughter. Shields, sensitive and proud, boiled with indignation. He found out who wrote the letter, leaped on his horse, started after Lincoln, and challenged him to fight a duel. Lincoln didn't want to fight. He was opposed to dueling, but he couldn't get out of it and save his honor. On the day of the duel, the Seconds interrupted and stopped the duel. That was the most lurid personal incident in Lincoln's life. It taught him an invaluable lesson in the art of dealing with people. Never again did he write an insulting letter. Never again did he ridicule anyone. And from that time on, he almost never criticized anybody for anything.

When I was twenty-eight years old, I thought I was a hot shot in the company I was working for. I was a brass, bold, kick-the-doors-, confidant young man who got results. I had a female boss at the time who treated me like a younger brother. In today's environment, some things would fall on some form of harassment. She never called me Rich, but instead used the insulting nickname for Richard, "Dick." She did this because even though I got results the way I went about it, in her mind I acted like a "dick." I didn't connect with people in a way that she felt was needed for me to prosper in my career and if I refined some habits, I could be the charismatic leader she thought I could become. She gave me a book for my birthday, <u>How to</u> <u>Win Friends & Influence People</u> by Dale Carnegie. I remember opening the gift and saying to myself, I don't need to read this book, I'm a star around this place with the results I was accomplishing. A few weeks to months went by and she kept pestering me to read it. Finally, I did, and the book became the most transformative moment of my business career. Not only did it expose me to all my faults but provided a clear path for me to change and still achieve wonderful business performance.

It's been decades since that gift. And yes, I still am in contact with that boss. And yes, she still calls me "Dick." Every day I try to be the person that is exemplified in that book and yet not every day do I live up to the ideals. I am Italian after all! 😊 I still am indebted to having a person who provided me critical feedback and turned my professional life around. As with Lincoln, I had a pivotal moment I could look back upon and pinpoint the moment of change when I could become proud of the person I am striving to become.

Moral

Changing things is critical to growth

Have you had a moment in your life that can be considered transformative?

____

____

____

Can you recall a time when you received critical feedback that resulted in a surprise?

____

____

____

As you assess your own Strengths & Weaknesses, what is something you can do to improve both?

____

____

____

What is a critical situation you face in the coming week and instead of providing criticism to an idea you can work collaboratively with others to improve the idea?

____

____

____

34

BITS & PIECES - HOW DO YOU MEASURE INTELLIGENCE?

After physicist Richard Feynman won a Nobel Prize for his work, he visited his old high school. While there, he decided to look up his records. He was surprised to find that his grades were not as good as he had remembered, and he got a kick out of the fact that his IQ was 124, not much above average.

Dr. Feynman said that winning the Nobel Prize was one thing, but to win it with an IQ of only 124 was really something. Most of us would agree because we all assume that the winners of Nobel prizes have exceptionally high IQs.

When I was a freshman in college, my parents came for the Fall Parents' Weekend and happened to meet my chemistry professor. He related easily to my father who was a high school teacher. He told my parents that I had a delightful personality, but I was enjoying the good life too much to get a degree in chemistry. My father being an educator could not wait to confront me on his disappointment that I was not focusing on what I needed to do. At this time, my two older sisters were in college and I made the third person and on a teacher's salary, my dad could not afford to pay my college fees. Therefore, tuition and board were 100% my responsibility and I maintained jobs all the way through my college life. I told my dad; it is not your concern it's mine! However, I took the challenge to prove my chemistry professor wrong. I graduated in four years with fourteen classmates who got degrees either as a major or minor in Chemistry. And yes, I did struggle. The ranking gap between 1 and 14 was likely pretty small, but the gap between 14 and 15 was big and I was easily number 15! Years would go by and my parents retired to my college town and subsequently became friends with my chemistry professor. It is a small world! Therefore, I would see him on visits to my parents and he occasionally would ask me to come and speak to students. My chemistry professor measured success by how many students he got to go on and get PhDs or other higher-level degrees and by that measurement was quite successful. Well after about six to seven years, only around five to six of my classmates were still active in the chemical field, after 10 years it had dwindled to around three to four and after fifteen years from graduating I was the only one in my class still in the chemical industry. All but four years of my career were in the lab, but I used my chemistry degree to get into a business capacity and eventually start my own company. I would tell my chemistry professor and his students in jest that Dr. Schmidt knows a lot about chemistry but still needs to learn a few things about human chemistry.

Moral

Don't judge a book by its cover or Judge yourself against your potential.

Do you think if Dr. Feynman knew his IQ was just a bit above average he would have had the audacity to launch creative research experiments that would win him the greatest recognition the scientific community can give?

____

____

____

Have you ever been told or felt that you are ordinary, and it influenced your decision to be audacious?

____

____

____

Most of us fall short of our potential because of self-defeating assumptions we make about ourselves, can you think of an experience where this held true for you?

____

____

____

What actions can you take this week to propel yourself forward on something or someone that is holding you back?

____

____

____

35

FRIENDSHIPPING

Athletes Martina Navratilova and Chris Evert were rivals on the tennis court. During the 1970s and '80s, the two played against each other eighty times over the course of sixteen years (sixty of those matches were finals). However, off the court, the two women developed a strong friendship that has endured to this day.

Navratilova was born in Czechoslovakia where she started playing tennis at a very young age. When she was sixteen, she began playing matches in the U.S. and met Evert not long after. "When I was a young girl, a long way from home, Chris and her mother [Colette] were always nice to me," Navratilova said later.

The admiration was and still is mutual. In another interview, Evert explained, "I think people forget that we were left alone in the locker room every Sunday after we played final matches, and one of us would be crying and the other would be comforting—nobody saw that." This translated to non-tennis settings as well. While Evert went through a divorce in 1986, Navratilova invited her to Aspen for a relaxing vacation. On that trip, Evert met her future husband: downhill skier Andy Mill.

I have benefited from many friendships in my life. One in particular was with a friend I met as a co-worker in a failing company. Several members of the leadership team had personalities that you wouldn't wish your worst enemies; however, the diamond in the rough was my friend KD. She later went on to become a representative in the State Government. She also was the first elected publicly gay person in a very conservative state. Over the years, we have had opportunities to keep our relationship intact. KD would often provide me with wise counsel, find opportunities to help me promote my business, and get introduced to key figures in the state. KD as you can now tell is one of those people who are givers and can see the light in all situations. As a twist of fate, Chris

Evert met her future husband by vacationing at her rival's home. I, too, had a twist of fate with KD.

Several years ago, my son came out as gay. As you can imagine the friendship that I had with KD proved to be a valuable beacon to assist our family to navigate through the journey to keep our home a safe, loving, supportive port to come home to.

Recently I compiled a list of twenty of the world's most inspirational people to me ranging from Nelson Mandela to Mother Theresa to Simon Peres and included on that list is my good friend KD.

Moral

Friends make your life story

What friendships do you have that have influenced your path in life? Reflect on a specific story.

____

____

____

Have you ever had to or should have let go of a friendship? Explain

____

____

____

What friends do you have that you still can call for advice? List the qualities of your friends and the subject matter of advice they provide.

____

____

____

Which one of your friends can you reach out to this week and be a friend in need?

____

____

____

36

THE TRADE

One day a boy, who has a bag of marbles, proposes a trade with a girl who has a bag of candy. The girl gladly agrees. But as the boy gets out his marbles, he realizes that he can't bear to part with some of them. Rather dishonestly, he takes three of his best marbles and hides them under his pillow. The boy and girl make the trade, and the girl never knows he has cheated on her. But that night while the girl lies fast asleep, the boy has no peace. He is wide awake, pondering a question that nags at him: "I wonder if she kept her best candy, too?"

I had a situation early in my career when I was hired at a new company and was expected to "compete" against a co-worker named John, of my age. John went out of his way to train me in everything he knew about how to perform the job. I often was taken aback and had questions in my mind about his true intentions. After a period, I realized his true intentions were simply to make me the best-performing employee I could be and by doing so the company performed better. Over the years, John rose through the ranks of the company eventually becoming the North American President of a foreign-owned company. After almost a decade, I left that company and a short time later started my own company. My relationship and trust with John continued to grow over time and his well-earned admiration has remained in place now for over thirty years. I consult with him at least quarterly to provide mentoring and wisdom to assist me personally but also professionally in leading my company. I not only have encouraged his philosophy of teamwork throughout my career but have benefited enormously from this approach.

Like that little boy, many of us walk through life plagued by the question "Have others given me his best?" but the question that we must answer first is "Am I giving others my best?"

Moral

"Above all, be your best self" or "The heart that gives, gathers"

Can you recall a time when you have given 100% to a professional relationship? Explain.

____

____

____

We often hear the phrase, "evil expects evil." Can you think of a situation where this applied in your life?

____

____

____

Can you think of a situation where you held back from working with others on sharing necessary knowledge? Why did you take this approach? How could it have been different if you shared more openly?

____

____

____

What relationship can you improve this week by having a collective sharing of knowledge?

____

____

____

http://www.dailytenminutes.com/2018/07/story-boy-and-girl-exchanged-marbles.html

37

THE SUITCASE

In 1970 Bernard Sadow, a luggage company executive, was dragging two heavy suitcases through an airport when he noticed workers easily transporting a large machine on a wheeled skid. Sadow wondered, "What if I put wheels on these suitcases?" That led to a protracted How to stage, which began with Sadow attaching four wheels to a suitcase laid flat. Providing a way to drag one's bags. But that idea was later improved by an airline pilot, Robert Plath. Who thought of using a long upright handle to pull the suitcase propped up on two wheels (instead of laying flat on four)? The end result of all that questioning by Sadow and Plath: the now-ubiquitous Rollaboard suitcase.

Innovation can come at unexpected moments, sometimes in the shower, in a dream, or perhaps in the middle of a catastrophe. My company implemented an idea into our industry that was surprising that it had not been done before. When municipalities are installing certain treatment technologies to remove iron and manganese from drinking water, the iron and manganese are in a dissolved form until it oxidizes and this then forms a solid. This material over time accumulates in the treatment vessel and needs to be backwashed out of the vessel in order to prevent a dangerous pressure build-up from occurring. We created a system called H2Zero to backwash the water into a container and collect the solids but also more importantly it provided an environmentally friendly approach to avoid wasting the gallons of water that traditionally are lost when you backwash a system. I do not believe our idea will have the impact naturally of the rollaboard suitcase but innovation moves us forward. As with many innovations, it starts with curiosity to improve something and asking "What if...?

Moral

Innovaion is usually a small improvement

What is one innovation that has occurred in your lifetime that has proven to be a game changer?

____

____

____

What have you been involved with in your company that has contributed to a new way of doing something?

____

____

____

How did you ever let an idea that you have died on the vine? What was it?

____

____

____

For the coming week or month, write down every new idea that you have, try to come up with at least 2-3 ideas a day for a week, or a month then keep going.

38

THE STORY OF TWO WOLVES

(https://urbanbalance.com/the-story-of-two-wolves/)

An old Cherokee is teaching his grandson about life. "A fight is going on inside me," he said to the boy. "It is a terrible fight, and it is between two wolves. One is evil — he is anger, envy, sorrow, regret, greed, arrogance, self-pity, guilt, resentment, inferiority, lies, false pride, superiority, and ego."

He continued, "The other is good — he is joy, peace, love, hope, *serenity, humility, kindness, benevolence, empathy, generosity, truth, compassion, and faith. The same fight is going on inside you – and inside every other person, too."*

The grandson thought about it for a minute and then asked his grandfather, "Which wolf will win?"

The old Cherokee simply replied, "The one you feed."

When I started my company and the journey since the Two Wolves that I have had to constantly stare down have been the type of culture we want to have in the company. My last two companies developed a high-pressure micro-managing environment to get results and the company I felt most comfortable with was at an earlier job where the atmosphere of teamwork and risk-taking were encouraged. In an earlier story, I discussed that we built my company around a Danish word called "arbejdsglaede" which means "Live happy at work." My partner in the business was "old school" and believed in a hierarchical organization chart with defined job titles and you were promoted because you worked weekends as well. Naturally, he has always struggled to fully adopt the arbejdsglaede culture initiative although he felt as if he was always supportive. Not every day is going to be a happy office day but having engaged empowered employees is certainly a different culture than the "old school" approach. In fact, at my company, we have a team called the HapE3 Team, with the E3 meaning engaged, empowered employees. We have traditions of awarding orange socks for employees that perform Standards of Excellence (SOX), we have a huge dry-erase Happiness Wall for employees to scribe or post content, we host monthly staff meetings to share company performance and our goals, we engage with employees through a weekly moral software survey called Heartcount to gather timely metrics. All these efforts help support the wolves we want to feed and ultimately allow our company to have higher employee retention rates than how our industry reports. In fact, in the last few years, we have had employee retention rates in the 96% range and our industry generally performs in the 80-90% range.

Whether or not it's your first time hearing the two wolves' story, it serves as an important reminder of the power we have over our choices, experiences, and emotions.

Moral

Whatever you feed will grow.

Think of a recent example where you felt like a victim of a situation. Did you blame others?

____

____

____

We often allow people to have control over us, can you think of a situation where this has applied to you?

____

____

____

What story can you point to in your life where you have fed the good wolf? What happened and what was the outcome?

____

____

____

In the coming week where you can invigorate yourself by focusing on making a shift to approach, you're your work with arbejdsglaede.

39

———

THE LETTER

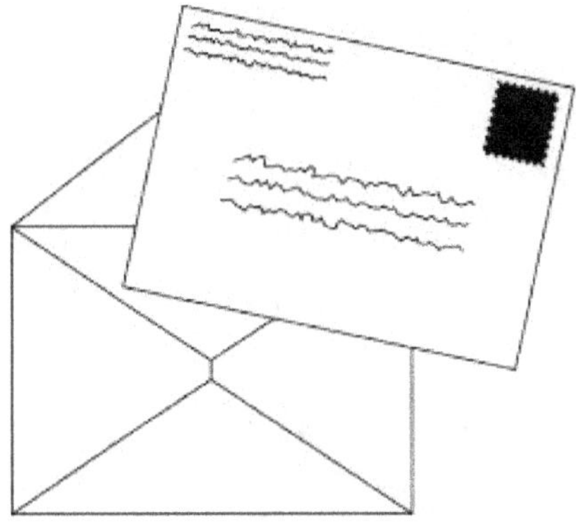

After seven days of protesting and three months of COVID-19, I came across a letter published in the Atlanta Journal-Constitution by a young girl Emerson Weber, 11 of Sioux Falls, South Dakota to her postman that somehow told a story better than any politician or pundit.

"I'm Emerson. You may know me as the person who lives

here who writes a lot of letters and decorates the envelopes. Well, I wanted to thank you for taking my letters and delivering them. You are very important to me. I make people happy with my letters, but you do too."

She didn't know his name, so she wrote on the envelope: "To Mr. Postman. This letter is for you. Yeah, you!"

Mr. Mailman (aka Doug, Emerson would find out) shared Emerson's letter with his supervisor, who shared Emerson's letter in the regional Postal Service newsletter. Later, Emerson watched Doug emerge from his mail truck carrying two boxes of letters, all for Emerson written by postal workers from around the country.

"A lot of them responded just saying they were thankful to me for reaching out," Emerson said. "One man gave me two pieces of his stamp collection. People are being really personal. I like it when they share about their families or a joke. I'm very personal in my letters, so I like getting personal responses."

Emerson's dad, Hugh Weber, was blown away. "I think they saw in her the willingness to be vulnerable, talking about her little brother and her love for Taylor Swift. They talked about their families, their hobbies, their pets, but also some aspects of loneliness and some aspects of feeling overlooked and a whole lot of gratitude for Emerson seeing them and acknowledging them"

I have always been fortunate to have people perform random acts of kindness to me. One recent event that stands out is with a young engineer named Janna, whom I hired many years ago out of GA Tech. She worked in the company for several years as an Applications Engineer and was developing quite nicely by adding additional responsibilities to her role. One day she came to me and discussed that she had another passion in life and that was to become a nun. After a few months of discussion and my encouragement for her to follow her calling, she made the decision to enter the convent. Then over the years, I would receive emails around Christmas or Easter telling me what she was doing. She always had her own aura of grace around her, and it was evident in her role as a youth leader that she was fulfilling what she had hoped. Her travels found her in NJ, a long way from GA.

When my mother died in WV, we had decided that we would hold her funeral back in NJ where we grew up, and in the Church, where all my siblings and myself were raised and married. It was almost twenty years since my parents had lived in NJ and we were expecting a small turnout at the church. The funeral had many lifelong neighbors and high school friends in attendance along with the entire family. While I was giving my mother's eulogy, I looked out from the lectern and my eyes locked on a familiar face. Sitting in one of the pews was Janna with her angelic face looking back at me. I had no idea how she would even know about my mom's funeral and while she never met my mom, I could feel the emotional comfort of joy she provided me. So as with Emerson, kind gestures happen and when they do, appreciate the miracle.

Moral

Kindness is such a beautiful thing

When was the last random act of kindness you received?
Gave?

____

____

____

Write down 1-2 memories you have of the moving kindness that you have received in your life.

____

____

____

Can you recall a recent event in your job where you have seen or participated in a Random Act of Kindness?

____

____

____

What is something you can do this week to surprise a co-worker with an RAK?

40

THE TEST

One night four college students were out partying late at night and didn't study for the test that was scheduled for the next day. In the morning, they thought of a plan.

They made themselves look dirty with grease and dirt.

Then they went to the Dean and said they had gone out to a wedding last night and on their way back the tire of their car burst, and they had to push the car all the way back. So, they were in no condition to take the test.

The Dean thought for a minute and said they could have the re-test after three days. They thanked him and said they would be ready by that time.

On the third day, they appeared before the Dean. The Dean said that as this was a Special Condition Test, all four were required to sit in separate classrooms for the test. They all agreed as they had prepared well in the last three days.

The Test consisted of only two questions with a total of one hundred points:

1) Your Name? __________ (1 Points)

2) Which tire burst? __________ (99 Points)

Options – **(a)** Front Left **(b)** Front Right **(c)** Back Left **(d)** Back Right

We are all familiar with the phrase "Shit Happens." In my company's twenty-year history, we have made many mistakes. Some of them were significant and of course, some resulted by accident. We had one painful experience with our first Food & Beverage project. The project called for stainless steel piping and since we have been used to doing stainless steel work on municipal projects, we built it as we would a municipal customer. We built and shipped the system and upon inspection by the beverage company's installation contractor, we used an incorrect weld. A $100K mistake! We had to hire a local welder to rework the welding, so it was in compliance. We owed up to the mistake and completely absorbed the costs, which included all our profitability and resulted in a loss on the project. The system started up and everything went fine. The beverage company was pleased with how we took complete responsibility for the problem and to our delighted surprise awarded us two additional projects within a year.

Moral

Take responsibility or you will learn your lesson.

What is the biggest mistake you have made in your professional life?

____

____

____

Can you recall a situation where you failed to accept full responsibility for a mistake?

____

____

____

"Honesty is always the best policy" Recall a situation where you in fact followed this advice.

____

____

____

In the coming week, what challenges do you face where you will be responsible for actions?

____

____

____

41

THE COOK

Once upon a time, a daughter complained to her father that her life was miserable and that she didn't know how she was going to make it. She was tired of fighting and struggling all the time. It seemed that just as one problem was solved, another one soon followed.

Her father, a chef, took her to the kitchen. He filled three pots with water and placed each on a high fire.

Once the three pots began to boil, he placed potatoes in one pot, eggs in the second pot, and ground coffee beans in the third pot. He then let them sit and boil, without saying a word to his daughter. The daughter moaned and impatiently waited, wondering what he was doing. After twenty minutes he turned off the burners.

He took the potatoes out of the pot and placed them in a bowl. He pulled the eggs out and placed them in a bowl. He then ladled the coffee out and placed it in a cup.

Turning to her, he asked. *"Daughter, what do you see?"*

"Potatoes, eggs, and coffee," she hastily replied.

"Look closer," he said, *"and touch the potatoes."* She did and noted that they were soft.

He then asked her to take an egg and break it. After pulling off the shell, she observed the hard-boiled egg.

Finally, he asked her to sip the coffee. Its rich aroma brought a smile to her face.

"Father, what does this mean?" she asked.

He then explained that the potatoes, the eggs, and the coffee beans had each faced the same adversity-the boiling water. However, each one reacted differently. The potato went in strong, hard, and unrelenting, but in boiling water, it became soft and weak.

The egg was fragile, with the thin outer shell protecting its liquid interior until it was put in the boiling water. Then the inside of the egg became hard.

However, the ground coffee beans were unique. After they were exposed to the boiling water, they changed the water and created something new.

"Which one are you?" he asked his daughter.

Many times, in my entrepreneurial career I was challenged with "do I give up or do I keep going?" One of the most pivotal days in my life occurred back in 2013. I decided to merge with another company a year earlier and things had gone poorly. The merger company failed to deliver on their expectations and the bank for which we had our Line of Credit gave us conditions that must be met in three months to keep the line in place. Some of the conditions were: that we needed to increase sales, cut expenses, remove the founders of the merger from the company, improve the balance sheet, and return to profitability. A tall task and yet we did it. The day arrives. The bank was scheduled to meet with me to address renewing the line, and I was feeling great. Thirty seconds into the meeting, they announced they were calling in the Line of Credit. Minutes later, I was interrupted in the meeting by a phone call from my sister telling me that my father had unexpectedly died. I refocused and pleaded my case to the bank, but they had their marching orders and wouldn't budge. So, a bad day just became even more horrible. The survival of the company truly hung in the balance. Adversity was surely knocking, and I could have pitched my tent but instead drew some strength from my dad and plowed forward. Eventually, with some creative negotiating, took a short-term loan from several shareholders and even used some of my own savings. This kept the company afloat and eighteen months later restored a banking Line of Credit... with another bank!

Moral

Success is overcoming overwhelming struggles or When life gets harder, get stronger!

https://wealthygorilla.com/best-short-moral-stories/

When adversity knocks on your door, how do you respond? Are you a potato, an egg, or a coffee bean?

____

____

____

Reflect on a personal struggle you have been challenged with. How has it made you stronger?

____

____

____

Describe a situation in your professional career where you have faced adversity but were able to endure the challenge and it resulted in something positive.

____

____

____

What is one adversity you faced this week and what are three things you can consider turning it into a positive outcome?

____

____

____

42

TWO SALESMEN

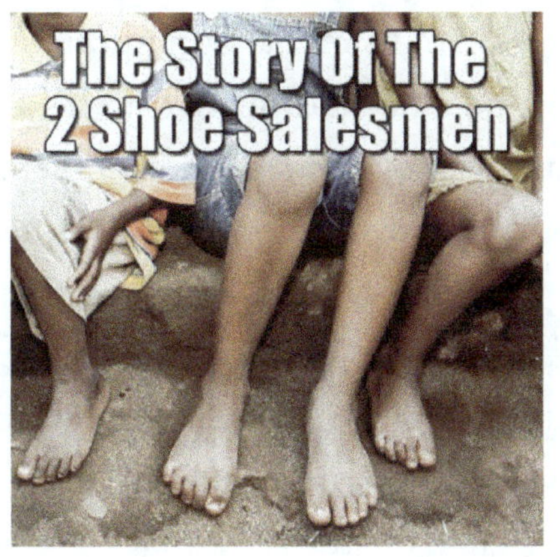

The following is a well-known motivational story about recognizing if someone is an entrepreneur or not. Two shoe salesmen from competing companies were sent to Africa to see if there was a market for their product. The first salesman reported back, "This is a terrible business opportunity, no one wears shoes." The second salesman reported back, "This is a fantastic business opportunity, no one wears shoes."

On the surface this seems like an easy enough story to choose who is right, surely the second salesman. However, probing deeper is much more likely to expose some business truths. I faced a similar question with regard to entering the Indian market. India is well documented for having one of the severest problems of arsenic poisoning in their drinking water and more people are drinking arsenic in their water than any other country. My company has earned a reputation as the market leader with the best technology and cost-effective solutions in North America. It's natural then to look upon India as the second salesman in Africa. It's a fantastic business opportunity. However, ethical business practices, integrity of product performance, safety, regulatory approvals, foreign-owned business, working capital, and cost of goods issues all thwarted our efforts to have the impact that was possible. In effect, both salesmen are correct but before jumping into optimistic opportunities quickly make sure you do your due diligence to study the market. Several years into our venture into India, we still have not been able to achieve the results we had expected and sadly the impact we could have on people's lives is greatly tarnished, and therein lies real life!

Moral

Most of us see, few observe

Which salesman are you? Why do you say that?

____

____

____

Did your answer change after reading my comments?

____

____

____

Can you describe a situation where either you ran into an opportunity quickly or not at all? What occurred?

____

____

____

Think of a few questions or research that needs to be done to better assess the opportunity.

____

____

____

What is something you are working on this week that is in need of asking more questions or getting more research done? Compile your list and share it with your supervisor, co-worker, or teammate.

____

____

____

43

MAN'S SEARCH FOR MEANING

One of the most inspiring books I have ever read is Victor Frankl's <u>Man's Search for Meaning</u>. If you are unfamiliar with this book, it involves Victor Frankl's internment in a Nazi Concentration Camp. In 1939 Frankl held a prestigious job as a psychiatrist in Vienna's Rothschild Hospital assisting patients in finding meaning in their lives even though they suffered from depression or mental illness. In 1942, the U.S. consulate in Vienna informed him he could immigrate to the U.S. Frankl decided to stay in Vienna for the sake of his aging parents. In September 1942, Frankl was arrested along with his family and spent the next three years in four different concentration camps. Frankl focused his time on helping fellow inmates find beauty in things, look for glimpses of humor or solitude, find inner freedom, and seek the steely resolve to avoid giving up. He most importantly realized that "no matter what happened, he retained the freedom to choose how to respond to his suffering." (pg 158) Although Frankl survived the concentration camp, his family including his parents, brother, and pregnant wife did not. Frankl returned to Vienna after the war with a sense of obligation to help his countrymen and the Jewish community to recover from the horrible tragedy of the Nazis.

The following is an excerpt from the book as told by William J. Winslade.

Once when lecturing, he was asked to express the meaning of his own life. He wrote the response on paper and asked his students to guess what he had written. After some moments of quiet reflection, a student surprised Frankl by saying, "The meaning of life is to help others find the meaning of their life." "That was it exactly." Frankly said. "Those are the very words I had written."

It's nearly impossible for me to find a life experience that can compare to Victor Frankl's. However, I like to believe the philosophy he taught resonates with me. Several years ago, for

Mother's Day, I built in the woods in my backyard a Serenity Path for my wife. The path is filled with fifteen or more thought-provoking quotes or signs, many dealing with nature, some homemade yard art, some wind chimes, bird feeders, benches, a stream, and a sitting area we call the overlook. As an accompaniment, we have eight different brochures which include five of the quotes in the path and questions of reflection that go along with the quote. One of the powerful quotes happens to incidentally be from Anne Frank, a teenager who happened to lose her life in a Nazi concentration camp. She says, "How wonderful it is that nobody needs to wait a single moment before starting to improve the world." During COVID-19 and the protests that came to light on police inequality against blacks, the high unemployment rates, and people bewildered by how things spiraled so fast, I placed a sign in the front yard on weekends and offered people in my neighborhood "free" tours. The reaction from neighbors was so heartfelt and at times we had tears of people being overwhelmed with joy. We estimated maybe between one hundred fifty-two hundred people came by, 95% I had never met before. In a small way, I believe I helped people find a glimmer of inner freedom and solitude. What I do know is, that neighbors we did not know are now friends.

Moral

Always help others (You might be the only one who does)

Which relationship in your life has had the most impact on you? Why was that?

____

____

____

Have you ever experienced a setback that in retrospect, brought you further in life? What happened?

____

____

____

What is your most recent life lesson? Were you ready for it, or did it come as a surprise?

____

____

____

What is an action you can take this week to help someone out?

____

____

____

44

THE STORY OF THE CHINESE
BAMBOO TREE

L ike any plant, the growth of the Chinese Bamboo Tree requires nurturing – water, fertile soil, and sunshine. In its first year, we see no visible signs of activity. In the second year, again, no growth above the soil. The third, the fourth, still nothing. Our patience is tested, and we begin to wonder if our efforts (caring, water, etc.) will ever be rewarded.

And finally, in the fifth year – behold, a miracle! We experience growth. And what growth it is! The Chinese Bamboo Tree grows eighty feet in just six weeks!

But let's be serious, does the Chinese Bamboo Tree really grow eighty feet in six weeks? Did the Chinese Bamboo Tree lie dormant for four years only to grow exponentially in the fifth? Or was the little tree growing underground, developing a root system strong enough to support its potential for outward growth in the fifth year and beyond? The answer is, of course, obvious. Had the tree not developed a strong unseen foundation it could not have sustained its life as it grew.

In 2010, I began an event that has continued until this day. I have three sons and my youngest at the time was thirteen years old. We were discussing an idea where I could build his vocabulary and at the same time provide some daily motivation. We discussed sending out a six-word or less phrase daily. Because I am in the water industry, we had settled on a name to call, "The Ripple Effect." We were walking into a hardware store to work on a school project, and my son said, "Dad, we need to get good wood?" With that, we changed the name to Goodwood. We felt it fit the principal better that a home is built on a strong foundation and needs good wood to build walls and structure or in other words a strong character. By 2020 we have had over 3,500 GoodWoods sent out via text every morning. Like the Chinese Bamboo Tree, I have been nurturing my sons and many others for over ten years. Some of them have sprouted certainly not eighty feet in six weeks but the growth is impressive. Coincidently, most of the morals selected in this book are some of the daily GoodWoods that have been sent out. See Rich Cavagnaro on Twitter to receive daily tweets.

Moral

It takes nurturing to grow up. Don't forget to Start every day with Goodwood 😊

P.S. – To see an amazing video explaining the miracle of the Chinese Bamboo Tree, go here to see Matt Morris' video » Chinese Bamboo Tree Video

https://www.mattmorris.com/how-success-is-like-a-chinese-bamboo-tree/

Maybe it's time to reflect on an old, old poem by Henry Wadsworth Longfellow that is as true today as it was when he wrote it over 100 years ago:

"The heights by great men reached and kept

Were not attained by sudden flight,

But they, while their companions slept,

Toiled ever upward through the night."

Progress takes time and is often slow, frustrating, and unrewarding, can you think of a similar situation in your life where it took years for you to finally reap a harvest?

What is something you have been patiently waiting for to happen? What are you doing to nurture the opportunity? Do others consider you foolish for waiting?

We live in a quick-fix society, we want to have it now, how does this mindset hurt or help you?

Think of something in your past where you stopped nurturing either an idea or pursuit. What happened? Why did you stop?

Take the time this week to prepare a five-year plan, think it through, and write down the actions you need to take to accomplish your goal.

____

____

____

45

UNSOLVED PROBLEMS

One day in 1939, George Bernard Dantzig, a doctoral candidate at the University of California, Berkeley, arrived late for a graduate-level statistics class and found two problems written on the board. Not knowing they were examples of "unsolved" statistics problems, he mistook them for part of a homework assignment, jotted them down, and solved them. (The equations Dantzig tackled are more accurately described not as unsolvable problems, but rather as unproven statistical theorems for which he worked out proofs.)

Six weeks later, Dantzig's statistic professor notified him that he had prepared one of his two "homework" proofs for publication, and Dantzig was given co-author credit on another paper several years later when another mathematician independently worked out the same solution to the second problem.

My partner in my business is the company's MVP! He has a talent for designing solutions to unsolvable problems. The most tremendous example of this is a project we did in California with multi-contaminant groundwater. The community was facing the loss of its biggest manufacturer, a cheese producer, if they didn't remove the contaminants and not only improve the taste and odor but the aesthetics as well. Several large water engineering companies had put together very complex and expensive suggestions to solve the community's problem. The town was under extreme pressure to come up with an answer and yet had failed repeatedly with the traditional approach. GG, my partner, was not going to be denied. He was able to provide a unique design approach coupled with various proven technologies in a novel layout Then when piloted, it proved to not only save the town multi-millions on the capital design and operating costs but catapulted my company to having our largest project ever. The naysayers were ever present by the large firms, GG ignored their concerns much like George Dantzig to solve an unsolvable problem!

Moral

Every problem has a creative solution

https://www.snopes.com/fact-check/the-unsolvable-math-problem/

We all have faced unsolvable problems or situations in our lives, reflect on one or two.

____

____

____

Do you know people who sometimes are so focused on solving a problem or involved in a situation that their lack of awareness of things going on around them becomes evident?

____

____

____

Who is your network of support that you have to help you solve your problems?

This week list a few unsolvable problems that exist in your life or work.

46

DANCE UNTIL IT RAINS-PERSISTENCE

Vic Johnson, author of the book <u>Dance Until It Rains</u>, begins with the story of a tribe in Africa that confounded all of the anthropologists. It seems that this tribe had for centuries enjoyed a 100% success rate with its Rain Dance. In comparing this tribe to other tribes who did rain dances, but who didn't always experience success, the experts couldn't find anything that differentiated the one tribe. They performed the same rituals, praying the same incantations to the same gods, in the same costumes. Like all the tribes, they sometimes danced for days, even weeks on end. Finally, an astute observer noticed something very telling. The successful tribe did one thing – and only one thing – different than the other tribes. They ALWAYS danced UNTIL it rained!

I've had success in my life by being very disciplined in setting goals and then being disciplined by daily actions, which fill up my weekly rhythm chart (WRC), and then build to my 30-Day Action Plan (30DAP). The WRC and 30DAP tie back to my annual goals. My annual goals are based on eight categories to help me have a full well-rounded life. Those categories are Spiritual, Financial, Physical, Mental, Relationships, Business, Family & Lifestyle. Around Christmas week, I take the time to reflect on the past year and then set the course for the coming year. I was inspired by the goal-setting process from a program titled "Designing the Best Ten Years of Your Life" by Darren Hardy. The goal template itself requires you to write down your SMART (Specific, Measurable, Attainable, Relevant & Time Sensitive) Goal, intermediate destinations required quarterly to stay on track, resources needed, mentors to help, research required, training necessary, and ten crucial actions that are needed to be accomplished with deadlines. Many people go through their years and lives and don't make the effort to put in this type of discipline. For me, this process works, and I apply it to my company goals. I'm proud of my track record of accomplishing goals and I know that track record is tied to my disciplined approach. Already, I can feel most of you are ready to move right past this exercise but success like the tribe in Africa happens when you are committed to a process.

Moral

Without a goal, you won't score

Can you think of a time when your persistence paid off for you?

____

____

____

Do you feel you benefit more from a structured approach to your life or more of a let life take me where it goes? Write down an example or two.

____

____

____

On a sheet of paper write two columns, one titled Things You are "Persistent" About and the other Things You are "Not Persistent" About. For each item, write down why you either are or are not persistent. Can you reframe the "Not Persistent" column with thoughts from the "Persistent" column to realize a different outcome?

———————————————————————

———————————————————————

———————————————————————

In the coming week reframe a current goal, is it a SMART Goal, what are your intermediate destinations, what additional research is needed, what additional training is required, who are possible mentors, and what are the critical actions required to take?

———————————————————————

———————————————————————

———————————————————————

If you would like me to share my goal-setting process, please contact me at rcavagnaro129@icloud.com

47

30,000 MORNINGS

This is your life; don't miss a day of it.

30,000 mornings, give or take, is all we're given. If you're 26, you still have 20,000 left. If you're 54, you still have 10,000. An accident or illness could change all that, of course. But let's count on you to remain safe and healthy all your allotted life—in which case you still have plenty of time...

sort of.

"We get to think of life as an inexhaustible well," wrote

composer and author Paul Bowles, who lived to the ripe old age of 32,442 mornings. "Yet everything happens only a certain number of times, and a very small number, really.

"How many more times will you remember a certain afternoon of your childhood, some afternoon that's so deeply a part of your being that you can't even conceive of your life without it? Perhaps four or five times more, perhaps not even that. How many more times will you watch the full moon rise? Perhaps twenty. And yet it all seems limitless."

30,000 mornings. We'll spend some of them on the treadmill, fighting traffic, or standing in line at the Starbucks store. Just be sure to spend some of yours seeking and savoring the real beauty, mystery, and adventure of your days. This is your life, your one and only life—don't miss a day of it.

There are people in our lives who just seem to transcend this philosophy. I hope people see me as a person who lives with an appreciation of enjoying life. In the past year, I had a remarkable set of events that resulted in my wife and I having a truly memorable set of days. I was attending a tradeshow in Denver and my wife and college-age son joined me after the tradeshow for a few days of vacation in the Rockies. It was mid-June and when we left Denver for a drive to Aspen, many roads were opening up for the first time that summer due to the considerable snowpack Colorado enjoyed that winter. We were on some roads that happened to be the first days they were opened, and we were able to have almost no traffic. The views and the wildlife and hikes were inspiring. We were making our way to Aspen which happened to coincide with

Food & Wine Magazine's Annual Aspen event. My wife, who prides herself as a "foodie," was overjoyed that we would be in the environment of the event but due to the price for tickets not participating in any of the cooking shows or the food and wine tastings under the large tents. We were happy anyway just being in Aspen, who wouldn't be? We enjoyed being in a few restaurants, and my wife would occasionally enjoy seeing a celebrity chef. In one particular restaurant, my wife asked if she could customize a meat and cheese plate, and they went along with her request. Soon the table next to us filled up with some folks from The Colorado Restaurant Association. They saw our platter and asked the chef if they could have one made as well. This led to instant conversations about the F&W event and immediate friendships. Minutes later, a well-known TV celebrity chef walks by sees the platter, and marvels at it. My wife is now feeling overjoyed. Aspen. As we continued conversations with our new friends, they clearly were able to see the joy my wife was experiencing by being at the F&W event. They said they were not attending the food and wine private tasting the next day, and we could have their passes. Shocked was an overstatement. We attended the events of private cooking demonstrations with celebrity chefs and then spent hours at the Food & Wine tasting event. We enjoyed a day of being the Rich & Famous and good fortune smiled on us, not just that day but the entire week in Colorado. Some days stand out more than others, but when you have an awesome day make sure you take the time to appreciate it.

Remember:

1) This is your life, and there is no such thing as an insignificant day.

2) Your days are far more valuable than your money.

3) You can always get more money, but you can never get more days.

An excerpt from the best-selling book, <u>"7" How Many Days of the Week Can Be Extraordinary?</u> by Dan Zadra and Kobi Yamada. Posted on October 7, 2014, by Dan Zadra Zadra Creative Blog

Moral

Make one of "those" days...Today!

What are you looking forward to?

____

____

____

When was the last time you felt really alive? What were you doing?

____

____

____

Do you know where you are on your journey?

____

____

____

If a week was eight days, how would you use the extra day? (Don't say catch up at work!)

____

____

____

Finish the sentence...this week I will....?

____

____

____

48

THE KITE

In 1855, the great Niagara Suspension Bridge was built by flying a child's kite across the 855-foot chasm. Attached to the kite was a string, attached to the string was a cord, attached to the cord was a rope, and attached to the rope was a cable—sure and strong.

Our world needs more kite-flyers and bridge-builders. If you have a big idea or a project in mind, step one is to take step one. Just fly your kite to the other side and go from there.

Big positive changes are seldom accomplished all at once; it's usually a matter of one step leading to another. What are you waiting for?

When I started our company, our first water treatment system was a filter at a flow rate of 0.5 gallons per minute. We then added a 1 gpm filter. Soon we expanded to a 5, 7.5, and 10 gpm system. After that, we grew our product line up to 100gpm. Within a few years, we had sold 300 gpm, and a few years later we had a design that reached 1 million gallons per day. Eighteen years from when the company started, we had the largest groundwater treatment system in the U.S. at 12 MGD. Our story is very similar to the kite attached to the string, attached to the cord, etc. It takes time to build a business, but every little step forward counts.

Moral

Take a step, then another step

What is something impactful in your life that has happened that started out with a small success/step?

____

____

____

Think of a project you participated in and list the steps that were required to bring it to fruition.

____

____

____

What movie example can you think of that parallels the story of the Niagara Suspension Bridge or the example I used in my story?

____

____

____

In the coming week, what is one big goal that you have for which you can write down three to five small steps you can take to move your goal forward?

____

____

____

49

THE MECHANIC AND THE SURGEON

A heart surgeon took his car to his local garage for a regular service, where he usually exchanged a little friendly banter with the owner, a skilled but not especially wealthy mechanic.

"So, tell me," says the mechanic, "I've been wondering

about what we both do for a living and how much more you get paid than me."

"Yes?" says the surgeon.

"Well look at this," says the mechanic, as he worked on a big, complicated engine, "I check how it's running, open it up, fix the valves, and put it all back together so it works well as new. We basically do the same job, don't we? And yet you are paid ten times what I am - how do you explain that?"

The surgeon thought for a moment, and smiling gently, replied, "Try it with the engine running."

Ah...this is the difference between thinking you could be an entrepreneur and actually being an entrepreneur. I want to put a different spin on this story and in my story it's the difference between working with a person employed by a large firm and their value vs my commitment and word as owner and CEO of my company. A tactic often used by large competing firms in our industry is to get the design engineer to include bonding on the job. This could be a situation for a small company to possibly have up to 3% additional costs to incur on a project. 3% may not seem much but to an industry that has many competitors, this is the difference between winning and losing. In order to offset a large portion of this cost, it is required that a small business owner has to put up a Personal Guarantee. Doing this changes the commitment I have to ensuring a successful project outcome. I can state rather assuredly that I, along with my staff, knew we would have a successful project. In my career, I'm proud of our record of achievement of never having a lawsuit or insurance claim on one of our projects. This in itself became a value-added statement we could use against our competition. So yes, as an entrepreneur the engine is always running.

Moral

Changing your view, changes your viewpoint

What is something you do that you know you are better at than most people?

____

____

____

What is the biggest risk you have taken professionally?

____

____

____

What has been one of your perceptions that you had that turned out to be incorrect or wrong?

____

____

____

What skills does your supervisor possess that would be beneficial for you to have to advance your career?

____

____

____

What can you do in the next week that can help add value to your company?

____

____

____

50

CLAP AND CHEER

A small boy was auditioning with his classmates for a school play. His mother knew that he'd set his heart on being in the play - just like all the other children hoped to - and she feared how he would react if he was not chosen. On the day the parts were awarded, the little boy's mother went to the school gates to collect her son. The little lad rushed up to her, eyes shining with pride and excitement. "Guess what Mom," he shouted, and then said the words that provide a lesson to us all, "I've been chosen to clap and cheer."

A proud story I was involved with as a parent was when my son was a high school senior. As a rising junior, my son was gaining momentum as an elite baseball player. He was batting cleanup on his high school team and was playing shortstop and played on a Top 10 nationally ranked travel team. He had his sights on playing college ball and the prospects were looking good. Unfortunately, toward the end of his junior year, he ended up having a second injury to his elbow, this time resulting in Tommy John reconstructive surgery. He spent the next fourteen months recovering. On the last game of his senior season, my son was given the clearance to play, if he played second base. All this time, a senior teammate of my son, who played baseball with him from third grade on and whose father was my assistant coach through many years of travel baseball, had not played a single inning all season. However, he showed up at practice every day doing all the things required by a teammate. Naturally, as parents, my wife and I were excited to see my son get honored with a start on his last high school game. When our team took the field, we noticed our longtime coach's son at second base and our son was on the bench. We were happy for our friend, of course, and in the last inning, my son pinched hit and got a single in his only at-bat of the year. After the game, when we asked our son why he didn't play the field as expected, he told us he told the coach to let his friend get the start because he earned it through his commitment to the team. Of all the baseball glory my son shared on a baseball field, never have my wife and I been prouder of him. He wanted to have the opportunity to "clap and cheer" for a teammate.

Moral

Make your attitude your greatest asset or Kindness is free and yet priceless

What random act of kindness have you done that has made you feel proud of yourself?

____

____

____

Of all the people in your life, which ones are the most important to you?

____

____

____

Which life lesson would you want to share with your fifteen-year-old self?

____

____

____

During the next week conduct at least one Random Act of Kindness and write down how you feel. See how long a streak you can make.

____

____

____

51

SAY YES

(Story from Ten published by Compendium)

Life doesn't come with a roadmap to follow, but the closest thing is probably the inspiring "Legacy Project" launched by Professor Karl Pillemer of Cornell University in 2006. He asked 1,500 older Americans who lived through extraordinary experiences and historical events to share with him their most important lessons life lessons. Though the participants had a wide variety of knowledge and perspectives, virtually all of them chose this as one of their most important pieces of advice:

Say yes to life and see where it leads you.

Say yes when things come your way. You will always regret the things you didn't do. Saying yes to life is really saying yes to yourself. "Yes" opens the door to new ideas and experiences, lets the light in, attracts kindred spirits to your journey, launches dreams and new beginnings, and spares you from later regrets. Sure "yes" leads to change, risk, adventure, and sometimes even trouble, but "no" usually leads nowhere.

The biggest yes in my life came from my wife naturally....but not on the question will you marry me instead when I asked her if she was up for me to start my own company? I had been considering the idea for almost a year when I was staring at three critical career decisions, stay with my failing company in Atlanta and hope for a miracle turnaround, take a job with my former stable company, and relocate back to New Jersey with a terrific salary and benefit package or start my own company. I went on a trip to an industry trade show and purchased some books about starting a company, including <u>How to Start a Business for</u> <u>Dummies</u>. I took the time at the tradeshow to assess the market and sensed an opportunity. Then I began to write a business plan. However, one giant question was would my wife go along and be accepting of the financial risk this would put on our family. I had just turned forty, and we had three children. One was about to start college soon. Financially it seemed daunting and I was giving up a sure thing by my former company (although a relocation back to NJ wasn't entirely attractive). I put forth my compelling case to my wife and she said, "YES!" The task was challenging, and I went almost a year without taking any salary yes it has been filled with risk, adventure, and trouble at times, however saying "yes" has also been exhilarating.

Moral

Say yes to life and see where it leads you.

What story in your life do you have because you said yes to?

____

____

____

We all have critical moments where we say "No" to an opportunity. What were the circumstances? Do you regret saying no?

____

____

____

Can you describe a time when your gut instinct turned out to be right? What happened?

____

____

____

Take a clean sheet of paper and write down on a sheet of paper your bucket list items you have for the next twelve months that you want to say yes to doing. Flip the paper over and write down bucket list items you have for the next twenty years.

IT'S A WONDERFUL LIFE

In Frank Capra's beloved Christmas movie, "It's A Wonderful Life," a penniless George Bailey (played by Jimmy Stewart) dies, believing that he was a failure. But a big-hearted angel named Clarence wisely allows George to go back in time and see how the lives of his friends and family would have been so much less had he not lived.

George Bailey's bank account may have been small, but he was a rich man. He quietly devoted a lifetime to being a loving husband and father, a caring neighbor, and a loyal friend. "Remember, George, no man is a failure who has friends," says Clarence. Seeing this for the first time in all its beauty and simplicity, George implores his angel, "Help me, Clarence, please, I want to live again."

"Strange isn't it, George? Each man's life touches so many other lives. When he isn't around, he leaves an awful hole, doesn't he?" Clarence the Angel.

From One Life

My wife and I have been hosts to six individuals and families over the years. It started with our good friends who experienced some hard times and had to leave Georgia and move to California while their daughter was in her senior year of high school. At the time we too, like George were penniless as I was in the early stages of starting my company. She ended up living with us until she graduated from college. She became the daughter of a house of three boys. Next, we had a foreign exchange student from France intern at my company to assist a close friend whose executive son wanted a place abroad for his son to have while in college. Then we hosted a person from India for a few months who was coming to work in my company via a stay in Tucson. After that, we had an intern at my company who was the son of a Chilean executive we worked with. We have another young lady from Chile who took full-time employment at my firm. Finally, a family from Chile as well that comprised three young girls under six, a husband who we hired, and his wife. They ran into delays with his housing situation and arrived on our doorstep on the first day of school and my wife is a schoolteacher. Timing is everything!

The young lady from Chile happened to be extremely bold as she moved to the United States and accepted a job in my company without ever being in the U.S. I had known her from working with her company in Chile. She left all of her family and friends to take on a new life in an unfamiliar country. She is a similar age to my son's and easily blended into the house. After staying a few months in the house, she ended up becoming part of the family and joined us on family dinners, holidays, and other occasions. She possesses a strong female spirit and had no problem calling out gender as well as cultural inequality issues in our lively discussions. On top of that, my wife was able to get another female voice in the house and I finally got a family member that loved conversation. 😊. While all these live-in experiences provided an easy transition arrangement for our guests, they richly rewarded my family with many cultural exchanges. We learned words such as voorpret, hygge, and most importantly sobremesa (they are worth pausing and looking up and then applying to your life). I know our guests have always expressed great admiration for what we did, and it makes my wife and I feel a lot like George Bailey. Upon reflection, at the time we had guests, we never realized how opening our house to help others was really a gift for my family. The joy that we received from increasing our family size has undoubtedly allowed us to lay claim that it is indeed, "A Wonderful Life."

Moral

Love life, it'll love you back

How would the lives of others you know be impacted if you were not in their life?

Which conversation have you had in your life that has had the greatest impact on you? Why was that?

"No man is a failure who has friends." How does this apply to you and your relationships?

Have you ever received an unexpected gift from doing something nice for others?

____

____

____

Take a moment this week to list all the people you interact with and write down a thought or two on how you can enhance your relationship with them.

____

____

____

What inspires you to get to know yourself better and to discover new things?

____

____

____

What would you like to find out about yourself?

____

____

____